KU-693-246

Dedicated to
The Playground Theatre in Chicago.
I hope we can sell this in the lobby.

About the CD-ROM

The CD-ROM for *The Actor's Guide to the Internet* contains:

- Software installers—a starter kit for the Internet—including
  - Netscape Navigator for Windows
  - Netscape Navigator for Macintosh
  - FTP Explorer FTP application for Windows
  - Fetch FTP application for Macintosh
  - WinZip—a decompression utility for Window
  - StuffIt Expander—a decompression utility for Macintosh
- Index of links to Internet resources for actors
- Link to *heinemanndrama.com* Web site

All of these applications can be accessed directly off the CD-ROM.

The system requirements are:

- Windows 95 or higher
- Power PC Macintosh

Have a question about any of our electronic products? Call or e-mail our tech support hotline: (800) 793-2154 or techsupport @heinemann.com.

Contents

Acknowledgments

Special thanks to Lisa Barnett for the suggestion for this book and to Carrie L. Kaufman, Nicole Bernardi-Reis, Katie O'Mara, and everyone at PerformInk for three years of Recurring Bits. It's all been grand fun and I've even avoided getting trapped inside chat rooms during the whole process of choosing lovely Web sites. And, of course, I thank my family. The first work I had submitted for publication was "Dog Flight" in 1979. It took twenty years but Kozlowski is finally on a book cover.

An Introduction to the Internet 1

F ads. Often when some kind of new technology arises, those that are most threatened by it label the new technology as a fad in an attempt to minimize the popular impact it may have. Sometimes they're dreadfully wrong. In the 1920s silent filmmakers thought radio was a fad. Then radio people thought talking pictures were a fad. Then talking picture makers thought television was a fad. And on and on and on. By the 1990s, however, there could be no mistaking the impact that the information revolution would make on the world. How many commercials do you see advertising products that are accompanied by *http://www.something.com?* It can be really annoying to see all that type at the bottom of the screen, and one wonders how many viewers see an ad for Pepsi and then immediately run to their computers to check out the Pepsi Web page. But it happens, all the time.

There are many people in film and theatre who are scared of the Internet. This book will show you there's nothing to be afraid of. Digital actors will not replace real actors. Rather, you can use the new technology in your hands to advance your career. Honest! I'll talk a little more about that later but first I'll explain where the Internet came from and why it's not going to take over your mind or make you obsolete.

If you want to learn more about the Internet, one site you can visit that I visited is The History of the Internet, located at *http://www.davesite.com/webstation/net-history.shtml.* There are other sites that explain what the Internet is and how it was built, but I'll go through it a little bit right now to give you a little background.

To give you a little idea of the enormity of the Internet, as of October 1998, there were approximately 91 million English-speaking Internet users worldwide and another 66 million non-English-speaking users. Projections show that by the end of the year 2000, there will be about 320 million users worldwide of all languages. That's a little less than 10 percent of the world's population. I don't know about you, but I call that growth.

To start off, think of the Internet as a network. Anytime more than one computer shares common information, it's a network. The Internet is simply the world's biggest network, millions and millions of computers connected to one another.

The Internet has a longer history than you might think. Many people hear the word *Internet* and think of the World Wide Web, the graphics-heavy division of the Internet that wasn't introduced until 1992. Actually, the Internet has existed in one form or another since the 50s.

The embryo that resulted in the Internet was born in 1957 when the USSR launched the satellite Sputnik. The United States responded by forming the Advanced Research Projects Agency to establish a U.S. lead in science and technology applicable to the military. Then, funds were allocated for the formation of a military research network so that if the United States were attacked by nuclear weapons, the military would be able to overcome decentralization and communicate with its weapons to respond in an equally "efficient" manner.

In 1969, a network was created with four nodes at four universities in California and Utah. In 1972, the first e-mail program was created. In 1979, Usenet—the newsgroup network—appeared, and in 1992 the World Wide Web was born. The Internet contains other networks such as Gopher in its gigantic hold, but I concentrate on three parts of the Internet in this book: e-mail, newsgroups, and the Web.

E-mail

E-mail is perhaps the easiest-to-use of the Internet and this book goes into detail about the best software to use for e-mail. Simply put, e-mail allows you to communicate with anyone in the world who also has an e-mail address. You no longer have to pray to the gods above that our post office will manage to deliver a letter, and you also have the advantage of instantaneous, relatively free communication. You don't have to wait for days to get an e-mail message.

Newsgroups

Newsgroups are message boards that center on a particular subject area. You can communicate with other users in a newsgroup by either posting messages to the boards in reply to their comments or by e-mailing them directly with responses and/or questions. It is one of the first systems developed on the Internet, relying on text only so the older, slower modems could handle it.

A similar communication tool that relies on instant "you are there" messaging is "chat," which pops up in different forms all over the Internet.

World Wide Web

The World Wide Web has only been around since 1992, but it has quickly become the most glamorous part of the Internet because of the integration of graphics and text. In the old days modems were too slow to reliably deliver actual images over phone lines. It would take hours to load some of the graphics you can load in seconds today. So while the history of the Web is only a small fraction of the history of the whole Internet, today it is the driving force in the constantly growing industry of online commerce.

Thanks to greater access to the Web by millions of people, those who run Web sites are now able to actually make money by either selling advertising space on their sites or by simply selling products from their sites. More and more sites like HotBot and Buy.com are advertising on television because they can now afford to advertise on television. Of course, not everyone is able to take advantage of these online buying opportunities. With only 91 million English-speaking Internet users, the pool from which online commerce sites can lure customers is much smaller than that of television and actual stores.

But people who have computers often have money. People who have money buy things. And advertising Web sites on television means that people who buy things will see those ads and visit those Web sites, and so on. Why am I mentioning this? Because it simply shows that the Web is indeed a powerful and influential force in the galaxy, regardless of how few people currently use it.

UNDERSTANDING THE WORLD WIDE WEB STRUCTURE

Since the World Wide Web is the focus of most Internet users and the most valuable resource for information on the Internet, it is the primary focus of this book. It may seem intimidating at first to enter a world where you have 340 million options, but the structure of the Web is set up so that even an *actor* can learn how to use it in a very short time.

The core of the Web exists in hyperlinks. Hyperlinks exist as highlighted text or graphics that, when you click on them with a mouse, take you to another Web page. Any one Web page can have hyperlinks to hundreds of other Web pages, and those Web pages can each link to hundreds of other Web pages. There were about 340 million Web pages as of November 1, 1998, and that number grows by at least a million every month. That growth is surely going to accelerate.

When I discuss Web sites, I am referring to a series of Web pages linked to one another that fall under one domain or subject. Let's take CNN Interactive. If you watch CNN, you often see *http://cnn.com* on the bottom of the screen in their advertisements. That is known as the URL or uniform resource locator, which is just a fancy Netspeak way of saying "address." (To help you keep track of the any URLs I mention throughout this book, I have listed them all by chapter in Appendix 1, p. 119.) Entering that URL will take you to CNN's home page, from which you can link to dozens of Web pages under the CNN umbrella. While it all seems simple enough, the challenge for the person programming the page is to make it easy for you to get back to the home page from wherever you are. Imagine a diagram linking the home page to ten other pages. Each one of those pages links to ten other pages and so on. The diagram looks an awful lot like a web, doesn't it?

NAVIGATING THE WORLD WIDE WEB

"Surfing the Web" refers to the often useless practice of blindly following hyperlink after hyperlink until five hours later you've wound up at a Saint Bernard appreciation site after starting out on the CNN Web site. Surfing is not something you want to do if you wish to have a life. It is best to have a solid idea of exactly what you're looking for. Speaking from experience, I can vouch that surfing can result in many lost hours much like a savage session of Super Mario Brothers can.

Hence, this book. That's why we're here. First, I'll explore the benefits of going online. Why should you care? Actors have acted for centuries without the Internet. Why should an actor go through the trouble of getting on the information superhighway? In the following chapters, you'll find it's no trouble at all. After making the inevitable decision to check out this Internet thing, you'll see just how to get on the Internet and why America Online may be the easiest way to get online but not necessarily the *best*.

After getting online and taking your first tentative steps on the Web, you'll learn about search engines and directories and how they can make your online experience infinitely easier, helping you find precisely what you're looking for on the Web and in newsgroups, too. It's better than surfing—trust me.

Given the constant change in the Internet, new sites that deal with all the subjects in this book could appear every day. From the moment the last word is typed in this book to the moment it arrives in your hands, Web sites will emerge that will equal or surpass those that are discussed here. That's where search engines and directories come in.

Once you learn how to find what you're looking for, you'll be given a course in Web sites that will help you as an actor, from sites that will help you get the proper training to sites that will help you get cast in film and television.

Finally, you'll learn the first steps to creating a presence on the Internet by building your own Web site. While having your own Web page as either an actor or part of a theatre company is not crucial to your success, it's still a great way for you to promote yourself or your organization, and you'll see the various ways you can go about creating that online presence.

But first you ask, "Why should I care?"

Why You Should Care

*E*very day you hear a new commercial on the radio advertising a Web site like Sidewalk.com or Buy.com or you see a new commercial on television advertising Yahoo! or HotBot and you really want to ask the whole world, "Who cares?"

You do. No, really. You *do*. You're the one who bought this book about the Internet. The Internet is vast. It is important because it is vast. It is not controllable by one corporation or one government. Anyone in the world with a modem and a phone line can access it. Of course, you need a computer with the modem, but that's beside the point.

As an actor, it's important to realize that the Internet provides the ultimate source of information. Simply by dialing a phone number you have limitless opportunity for knowledge. Knowledge leads to power.

So why, as an actor, should you decide to explore the Internet? Perhaps you already have a computer and already use the Internet. You may use it for e-mail or you may think only very lonely men use the Web to download pictures of movie stars.

Untrue. That's why this book is here. As an actor, whether you're in L.A., New York, Chicago, or Paducah, Kentucky, you can't ignore the Internet. Here's why:

- *The Internet gives you faster access to information than ever before.* Later on in this book I'll take a look at the home pages of Actors' Equity, Screen Actor's Guild (SAG), and the American Federation of Television and Radio Artists (AFTRA). Each site has information on how to join those unions, information that at one time you had to research either by calling the unions or by siphoning it out of your fellow actors. Now, all you have to do is type in the URL of said union and you have your information. And if the Web site does its job, it features much more than just information about how one joins the union. For example, earlier this year the SAG site opened its front page with updated news on the member vote that took place in January 1999 on the proposed SAG–AFTRA merger. The site functions as an up-to-the-minute resource for members as well.

  You can see these kinds of features on many of the Web sites you're going to read about in this boook. On the Internet, you can find a wealth of information more quickly than ever before. Subjects that used to be relegated to a very small group of individuals have been thrust into the international spotlight. Unfortunately, those subjects that have received the most publicity have to do with pornography. But the Web has much more to offer. Take as an example a subject I have a great deal of interest in: silent films.

  As an art form that has been dead for seventy years, the silent film spent decades regarded as a joke, considered antiquated and unimportant. Old cans of films were allowed to deteriorate and the art of silent film was in danger of disappearing forever. In the '60s, film historians and preservationists began to discover the rare beauty of silent films, and the easy access to 8mm and later video allowed whole new generations of enthusiasts to appreciate it. Over the past three years, the number of Web sites devoted to silent film has skyrocketed, and the New York Times even had an article on the increasing popularity of silent film, attributing much of it to the Web.

  Now silent film is a very specialized interest. Never again will it really capture the imaginations of millions. However, everyone has access to information about it and the opportunity to discover it. This is the case for millions of topics. There are Web sites about everything from the Australian cattle dog to the great Cardiff Giant hoax in New York in the 1860s. And if there are subjects that aren't represented on the Web, chances are someone has realized that and is making a site for one of them now. As you will see later, creating a Web page is an extraordinarily easy thing to do.

As an actor, you have many interests that, in one way or another, lead you on your path to a successful career. The Internet has a multitude of resources that you can take advantage of no matter what stage your career is in. For those of you entering the acting realm for the first time, there are Web sites for just about every college and university in the nation as well as all the leading actors training centers. For those of you who are deep into debt and your acting career, there are online guides to auditions, casting information, and further training.

- *The Internet is always growing.*
At last count, there were 340 million Web pages. Since this manuscript went to the publisher more Web sites for actors almost certainly have popped up. Someone might read this book and be shocked there aren't more Web sites that provide an online resource for monologues and decide to create a Web site for just that purpose, and so the Internet grows again.
- *The Internet gives you a chance to commiserate with actors worldwide.*
The online community is weighed toward those actors who have either enough money to buy a computer, are fortunate enough to be allowed to use computers at work for leisure purposes, or are lucky enough to have received a computer as a gift. So, as in all Internet communities, the actors you find on the Net will be a little more computer savvy and often more affluent than other actors.

Still, with immediate access to a world full of fellow humans whom you would otherwise never know, the Internet provides you with the greatest chance to meet new people from across the continent than ever before. Newsgroups and message boards allow you to exchange information and ideas. Your ability to become a Webmaster—someone who makes Web pages—and to communicate with other Webmasters is greater than you think.

And, let's not forget that the Internet is pretty fun, too.

How to Get Online 3

*T*he process of getting online is a lot easier if you have a day job and you have Internet access at work. But getting a job simply because it gives you Internet access isn't really a good enough reason, is it? So let's assume you need Internet access at home because you're fabulously successful as an actor and don't need a day job in an office. The first thing you'll need is a computer that will enable you to access the Internet.

Your computer can either be a PC or Mac. The PC market is the one dominated by Bill Gates and Microsoft. Since they dominate the market, any computer you have used in the past most likely contained the Windows operating system from Microsoft. The main advantage of a PC is that because they dominate the market, there are more choices of general software out there for you. The main disadvantage is that PCs are known as "memory hogs," meaning the Windows operating system uses a lot more memory than the Mac operating system, making things slower. Also, because there are so many ports and connections that you have to make, simply putting together your computer might be a lifetime project.

Generally, you want to make sure you don't have a lot of wasteful hardware and software on your PC, so the best thing to do—rather than blindly buying a computer off the

9

shelf of a big appliance store—is to order directly from a manu-facturer like Dell at *http://www.dell.com* or Gateway at *http://www.gateway.com* and customize the features you need.

Meanwhile, over at Apple, *http://www.apple.com*, the Mac is the favorite of graphic designers and advertising agencies the world over. The Macs, especially the new iMacs with the colored transparent shells, are incredibly easy to operate, and much of what Microsoft has done with its Windows is a copy of the Mac operating system in its ease of use. And while Mac software is not as easy to come by as PC software, online commerce sites are emerging all over the place that may change that. The Apple Web site proclaims "iMac far outperforms other low-cost computers; its processor humbles the Pentiums in office PCs four times its price. iMac is easy to buy (it comes complete with everything you need). Easy to set up (there's no step 3). Easy to use (one click and "hello, Internet"). And designed to make you want to "reach out and touch it."

Whether you choose to buy a PC or Mac, when deciding what modem you want on your computer, you need to ask your-self how important speed is in determining your choices for Internet access. If you are going to be an infrequent Internet user who gets goes online for less than five hours a week, sim-ply using a phone line will be fine. The fastest modem currently available on normal—otherwise known as "analog"—phone lines is a 56K modem. That's approximately 56,000 bytes of information going through the phone line to your computer each second. Impressive, isn't it? However, because of network traffic and the traffic on phone lines, the maximum speed of these modems is really closer to 53,000 bytes per second. And, you may not even make it to 53K. It's a long, complicated tale of technobabble, but suffice it to say, if the phone lines in your area are not configured properly you may not make it past 33.6K! Fifty-six minus thirty-three is twenty-three, and that's a significant difference. If your phone lines can't support a 56K modem, you should settle for a 33.6K modem, which is pretty inexpensive, under $100.

Another note about 56K modems: When they were first made available to the public there were two different manufacturers that released two different versions of that speed. There were the X2 modem and the K56Flex modem. Some Internet service providers would provide dial-up access for optimum speed on one kind of modem and not on another kind of modem. However, recently a new standard has been set for 56K modems—the V.90 standard. All new computers feature V.90 modems, which should make things simpler. If you get a computer with either an X2 or K56Flex modem, there is a way to download an upgrade to V.90 from the modem manufacturers' Web sites. If you buy a 3com modem, for example, you can go to *www.3com.com* and they'll give you instructions on downloading what they call a "patch file" to upgrade the modem.

If you expect to be on the Internet more than five hours a week, you might want to consider faster alternatives to your normal phone line. These include ISDN connections, cable modems, or—to get really expensive—T1 connections. An ISDN line is simply a digital phone line that you use at speeds of 64K or 128K. ISDN lines require you to get a special modem that has capabilities beyond 56K modems. As you would imagine, these modems are more expensive.

ISDN modems cost upwards from $175 and often run much higher depending on the speed of your ISDN line. There are two basic speeds available: 64K and 128K. You end up having to add an entirely new phone connection—a digital one—and have to buy that new modem. If speed is what you need, then that's your answer.

Cable connections can go as fast as 1 MB per second, but it depends on whether your local cable provider offers that service. Most local areas have only one cable provider and if yours doesn't offer this, then you're simply out of luck. Cable modems are expensive, but some (like my local carrier 21st Century in Chicago) offer cable modems for rent.

DSL Connections (Digital Subscriber Lines) run about $200 a month to maintain as a service, and the modems are expensive as well. You get an incredibly fast connection but the cost is prohibitive unless you want a dedicated (constant or permanent) connection to the Net. The same goes for T1 connections. These give you direct connections to the Web via Ethernet cards. Unless you own a company with Internet users who need to be on the Web all the time and need the instant gratification of an incredibly fast connection, it's really not worth that kind of cost to you.

There are two options for getting on the Internet. You can utilize either an online service or an Internet service provider. You may say to yourself, "Hey! Sounds like the same thing!" Well, they're not. Trust me.

Online Services

Online services are self-contained, monitored networks that give you access to normal Internet features like the Web and e-mail, but their focus is their own created online community center. They often appear in your mailbox in the form of CD-ROMs that promise 100 free hours in your first month of membership, which would require you to be online an average of three hours a day, which is never recommended. America Online, or AOL, is the most famous and powerful of these services. CompuServe, Prodigy, and the Microsoft Network are a few of the other well-known online services. While AOL, among others, has worked hard to give the appearance of integrating more with the Internet, it really stands alone.

The content of an online service, besides its Web browser and e-mail and Usenet access, is controlled by one source. This is an advantage in the sense that you know exactly who to call regarding content on AOL or CompuServe. It's also very user-friendly. You don't have to search hard for content when you're using an online service. It's all laid out for you. America Online, for example, features a list of their "channels" from Games to News right on the screen when you first sign on. Online services also feature chat rooms on varying subjects so you can enter a given "room" and chat away with total strangers.

According to their Web site, America Online was founded in 1985 and has more than 12 million subscribers. It bought its nearest competitor, CompuServe, in 1998 and continues to grow as an advertising power and a center for all kinds of interactive events. There's something cozy and familiar about the community environment that AOL offers when you sign on but also something a little too "Big Brother" that could turn off the more fiercely independent actors out there. Also, because phone lines were never constructed to handle the kind of traffic that exists now, AOL is forced to expand its network constantly to compensate. So using AOL is a little like driving the highways in a major urban area. There's ongoing construction on the roads and by the time highways A through F are repaired, Highway A needs to be repaired again. For example, in August 1996 the service was completely down for nineteen hours. In the beginning of 1997, when AOL switched from a per-hour paying schedule to a flat monthly fee, usage increased at such a rapid pace that phone lines were constantly busy and e-mail service was disrupted. Now, AOL has expanded its network, but given the enormous growth of the Internet and the limitations of existing phone lines, that sort of problem can arise again.

Also, AOL's Web browser has always run behind Internet Explorer and Netscape in supporting animations and more advanced Web pages. The recent AOL/Netscape merger will make Netscape the browser in AOL, but you'll have to upgrade to whatever new version of AOL will support that, meaning a long download time.

Internet Service Providers

Internet service providers, ISPs for short, simply provide you Internet access with few bells and whistles. As you've read before, the Internet is a network that is not controlled by a central source. It's anarchy that has somehow managed to exist rather well. Internet service providers give you a phone number your modem can dial to access *their* connection to the Internet. ISPs often have host Web pages that give you some sort of guide to the Internet, but that's where the assistance often ends. The standard cost of basic service is $19.95 a month—and they often just charge your credit card first unless you request to pay by check.

When you go through the process of choosing an Internet Service Provider, it can get pretty confusing. The simplest way is to purchase either a Netscape Communicator or Microsoft Internet Explorer CD-ROM. (A copy of Netscape Communicator 4.5 is included on the enclosed CD-ROM for both Mac and PC users.)

Nationwide ISPs pose somewhat of the same problem as AOL in that there are many users around the nation using the systems, so the ISPs have to go through constant system upgrades, often *after* their users experience difficulties. However, like AOL and other online services, no matter where you are, you can almost always find a local access number to dial for service, which means to phone call is free. That's a big plus.

It takes a little more work, however, to find an Internet service provider that originates in your neck of the woods. You might want to consider starting out with an easy-to-use online service like America Online and use it to surf the Web for an Internet service provider that suits your needs, which is what I did. Many local service can provide you a more personal touch, although of course that depends on the individual provider. There are fewer users on local ISPs so there isn't nearly as much network traffic on them. Also, you can often get through to human customer service representatives more quickly than you can with large providers.

For example, I called customer service for the Concentric Network, a large nationwide ISP based in California and was put on hold for twenty-five minutes on a weekday at 5:00 P.M. Central time. I wasn't going to get any help on the phone. Concentric Network does have a feature on the Web site that allows you to chat online with a technician which partially compensates for a lack of voice contact, but you might be turned off by not being able to actually speak with a human being.

If you're connected already and want to check out reviews of dozens of ISPs, you can check out CNET's special review section at *http://www.cnet.com/Content/Reports/Special/ISP/index.html*. There's a search field that allows you to enter the name of an ISP and will return a grade compiled from a collection of votes based on several categories. The categories are reliability, e-mail, Web services, content and community, and technical support. If you don't know names of any ISPs, you can search for one by region. It's a very useful tool.

Another source of information is The List (*http://thelist.internet.com*). It labels itself as "the definitive ISP buyer's guide." It basically allows you to search the database by area. You can enter your area code, and a list of Internet service providers will come up. The list is basically a two column table outlines the features the ISPs provide. You can click on the name of the ISP and a single page for that ISP will come up with important information like a link to its home page, as well as phone numbers, hours of service, dial-up services offered, other services, and a comprehensive list of the fees that the ISP charges. While the site does not have any reviews of each ISP available, there is a link to important Internet related news, such as AOL's merger with Netscape. While these kinds of news items are not necessarily events that will directly affect you, it's still important when you join an online community that you're knowledgeable about the major players in the game.

When it comes to local Internet service providers, the software you receive won't be as easy to use as the CD ROMs for online services. Your access to software with a local ISP varies with each one. Often, the ISP provides disks with whatever browser it has signed a contract with, and after your computer is configured you can go through the process of finding the software that you want to use, whether it's a browser or e-mail program.

Web Browsers

A browser is a kind of software that allows you to view Web content. The difference between Web browsers is an important consideration. When programmers create Web pages, they have the option of including different programming instructions that only some browsers can read. You'll learn more about this when I tell you how to build your own Web pages. Suffice it to say for now that the same Web page may look radically different depending on the browser you're using.

Netscape and Microsoft dominate the Web browser industry. They have set the standard for all browsers that dare to compete. Each browser supports different program instructions, so words that might scroll across the screen on a Web page you view with Microsoft Internet Explorer might not scroll across the screen on Netscape and vice versa. This is one of the reasons for the "browser wars" you may have heard of, particularly in the Microsoft antitrust case.

NETSCAPE COMMUNICATOR
http://www.netscape.com

Netscape was founded in 1994, and like most companies that hit the Web just as it was exploding, the company quickly grew to possess the leading Web browser software in the world. The original Netscape Navigator could load Web pages more quickly than any other software and was the easiest to use. What gave Netscape the leading edge over other browsers was a licensing agreement with Sun Microsystems in 1995 to use its Java software. Without going into the technical specifications, suffice it to say that Java programs, called "applets," can create dynamic content on Web pages, and you could only view them with Netscape Navigator at the time. This gave Netscape a huge advantage and soon it cornered the worldwide browser market.

As of this writing, the most recent version of the Netscape browser was 4.5, defying expectations in the computer industry that demand new software versions go up one whole number. When Netscape Communicator 4.0, rather than just "Navigator," came out, it was redefined as an Internet suite, with a significantly improved e-mail program and newsreader program, allegedly erasing any need to get additional software for other Internet programs.

The best part of Netscape Communicator 4.5 is a button called "smart browsing" that gives you additional Web sites with content similar to that on the Web site you're viewing at that moment. It's handy if you're researching a given subject and want to see other sites regarding that subject as well. The program is not perfect and chooses sites based on other subjects contained within your site, but it's a great shortcut and a wonderful innovation.

Netscape has long been an innovator when it comes to plug-ins. Plug-ins are just what they sound like: pieces of software that you can install in the Netscape directory to give you a fuller, richer multimedia experience on the Web. One of the more popular plug-ins is Flash, from a company called Macromedia. It is a very fast loading and dynamic animation software that enables you to watch animations during the course of loading them.

Since the release of Netscape Communicator 4.5, Netscape was purchased by America Online in a stock transaction valued at $4.2 billion. Up until then, Microsoft Internet Explorer was the default browser used with America Online software. This will presumably change. As of this writing, the merger was expected to be finalized in spring 1999.

Microsoft Internet Explorer
http://www.microsoft.com/ie

When Microsoft unveiled Internet Explorer with Windows95, it was nowhere near Netscape Navigator in quality but when it introduced IE 3.0 in 1996, the browser wars began. Microsoft had its own version of Java and its browser became very comparable to Netscape's in scope and quality. The advantage that Microsoft has, of course, is that it runs everything. Because the operating system—otherwise known as "software that makes your computer go"—is Microsoft-run, it's often easier to run Internet Explorer within the context of what you're doing, especially if you run the Microsoft Office software, which integrates Internet Explorer by allowing you to link to Web pages from Word and Excel documents. Apple has also signed up to make Internet Explorer the default—automatic—browser for its new operating system.

The most current version of Microsoft Internet Explorer, as of this writing, was IE 4.0, and as much as I hate to admit it, it's pretty good. One of my favorite aspects of Internet Explorer is its ability to allow a Web page to take up your entire computer screen, getting rid of the oversized tool bars that get in the way of attractive Web pages. It allows you to see as much of the artwork without having to scroll down as possible. It's not the most groundbreaking feature in the world but I like it. It also allows you to subscribe to channels of content from providers like ESPN and set your computer to automatically dial up your ISP in the middle of the night, download news and information, and then disconnect.

As one could imagine, Microsoft has been sued several times for having so much power. At the time of this writing, the Justice Department was investigating Microsoft, and the result could be a breakup of Microsoft similar to the breakup of AT&T that occurred in the '80s.

But outside all the litigation, one must admit that Internet Explorer is an excellent browser.

OTHER WEB BROWSERS

There are other, smaller browsers that offer an alternative to the more well-known powerful ones. A great guide to these "rebel browsers" exists on CNET online at the following URL: *http://www.cnet.com/Content/Reviews/Compare/Browsers5/index.html*. To save you the time of going to your computer, turning it on, dialing the Internet, and checking out this page, I'll give you a little more information on some of these "rebel browsers."

Opera
http://www.operasoftware.com

The best aspect of this browser is that the file size of the installation file is only 1.2 MB. That takes a lot less time to download than Netscape or Internet Explorer, which run from 10MB to 15MB apiece depending on how many goodies you choose to include. A small file is particularly helpful if you have an older, slower computer that has little hard-disk space left. Opera lets you see most of what you need to see on the Web. It does support plug-ins such as Macromedia Flash.

Lynx
http://www.lynx.browser.org/

Lynx is an all-text Web browser that comes in handy if you have an old computer and/or old modem that simply cannot handle the fancy animations and graphics that come through the Web. The main drawback to Lynx is that so many Web pages feature so many graphics that they don't bother presenting an all-text version of their pages, meaning you can't view them at all. However, many of the bigger Web pages feature all-text versions that Lynx users can view

E-Mail and News

NETSCAPE MESSENGER

Netscape Messenger is the e-mail and news program included in Netscape Communicator 4.5. It is a vast improvement over the e-mail programs in Netscapes 1 through 4. It's now laid out much like all other e-mail programs, with a series of folders aligned vertically on the left side of the window and the right side split into two horizontal sections. The top right section lists incoming e-mails, complete with subjects, that you can have arranged by date, by sender, or subject. The bottom right field is where the body of the message will appear once you highlight the message subject in the field above.

Most e-mail programs are designed this way and Netscape finally caught up with the pack with this e-mail program. It provides a message filter that can send any e-mail from a specific person to a specific folder or even messages that contain specific words to a specific folder. It's a slowly advancing feature, although there aren't any foolproof "spam" features yet.

Spam is the term for any e-mail sent to multiple users, usually to advertise something. If you give away your e-mail address to too many people, you'll get on too many mailing lists, and you may get spammed. Watch out!

Messenger's newsreader is standard, a redesign from past newsreaders that Netscape has bundled in its Communicator suite. It's a part of Messenger, and treats newsgroups as mailboxes like "Inbox" and "Outbox" do. When you first access your news server, you have to download the names of all the thousands of newsgroups out there, which takes a while but those names then remain in memory, and you can search by keyword for newsgroups that you want to subscribe to. I'll say more later about specific actor-oriented newsgroups.

MICROSOFT OUTLOOK EXPRESS (AND OUTLOOK98)

Microsoft's new Outlook 98—part of its Office suite, which also includes Word, Powerpoint, and Excel—and Outlook Express, which is included in Microsoft Internet Explorer, allow you to check more than one e-mail account at once. This is very useful for someone like me who has a personal e-mail address, an address at my day job, and an address with my theatre company. While with Netscape you have to open the program and log in under a separate "profile" in order to check each different e-mail account, Outlook 98 (and Outlook Express) allow you to check mail on all accounts with the single press of a button.

Outlook Express allows you to filter spam. You can set the program to move spam to the "Deleted Items" folder so you never have to look at it in your Inbox.

EUDORA
http://www.eudora.com

Eudora is a popular e-mail program that has ruled the roost for years. It exists in two versions. There's a freeware version, which you can download and keep for free, called Eudora Light. You can get it from the Eudora Web site. There's also Eudora Pro, which you can purchase. There are many different products under the Eudora banner, which are owned by Qualcomm. The size of the downloadable file for Eudora Light is only 5 MB and that's a nice amount when compared to the 10 MB-plus Netscape and Internet Explorer files. Also, Eudora software is often thought of as a superior product because Eudora specializes in e-mail utilities rather than making them part of a larger Internet suite that specializes in its Web browser. Eudora was the first e-mail program to let you automatically send e-mails from certain senders directly to certain folders.

WEB-BASED E-MAIL

If you don't want to bother choosing an e-mail program, you might want to use one of the many Web-based e-mail options available. You basically go to the Web page, type in your username and password and retrieve your e-mail. This is particularly useful if you can access the Internet only at work and don't want to risk having personal e-mails detected from your work e-mail account. There are programs that a system administrator can use on an office network to detect e-mail reception as well as which Web pages you visit, so beware of surfing through Alyssa Milano fan pages during office hours.

These Web-based e-mail accounts are fairly free of spam, because the network is constantly guarded against it.

Web sites that feature e-mail include:

* Yahoo!: *http://www.yahoo.com*
* Excite: *http://www.excite.com*

- Hotmail: *http://www.hotmail.com*
- Rocketmail: *http://www.rocketmail.com*

Chat

Chat enables you to communicate with other Internet or online users while they too are online. Rather than communicating with another Internet user by e-mail, you can transmit messages to that user instantaneously. The user can then reply instantaneously, in effect creating an electronic conversation.

Depending on which service you're using to get online, you have a few options. Online services like AOL and CompuServe have their own unique chat features that allow you to communicate with other users of that service only although with AOL there is one exception in the AOL Instant Messenger Software. Chat rooms in online services follow certain subject areas, either created by the service or by the users themselves. Users congregate in chat rooms and the conversation begins!

In my opinion, chat rooms are almost entirely useless if you have more than a few people in the room and if those people are not truly committed to the subject at hand. If you want to create a chat room for you and your existing friends who live far away, it's a great way for you all to get together without actually getting together. Otherwise, you get a bunch of people in a chat room with their own agendas—sometimes twisted agendas—and the result is a kind of incomprehensible babble, like at the House of Commons on Sundays on C-SPAN.

On AOL you can maintain a "Buddy List" of friends who also use the service, to whom you can send "instant messages." You can also block other people from sending you instant messages.

If you're simply on the Internet, you can use Internet relay chat (IRC), which features channels that are much like chat rooms. These are more problematic in terms of content and control than the online service chat rooms, because they are not moderated like those services' rooms. Thus, a lot of questionable people are roaming around, and I really can't recommend IRC, unless you have set something up with people you already know to have some kind of conference together.

There are many different kinds of software available that offer access to IRC including Microsoft Chat but given that this is the last time I'll mention IRC, I won't go into detail about them.

AOL Instant Messenger and Mirabalis ICQ are two download-able programs that allow you to send instant messages to other users of the same service. The programs are free, and AOL Instant Messenger allows you to communicate instantly with users of both that software and America Online itself.

And, now, congratulations! You're online. Where do we go from here?

4 *E-mail and Newsgroups*

Once you get online you'll surely be excited about getting on the Web. But hold your horses! Most likely you've heard the hype about the information superhighway. If the Web is the superhighway, e-mail and newsgroups make up the side streets. They allow you to communicate with anyone in the world who is connected to the Internet. You can send an e-mail to someone on the other side of the world in a flash and even have online chats with him or her. One of the challenges, of course, is finding all these fellow creative types around the world. The ability to do that is there. You just have to know where to go to find them.

E-mail is a fairly simple tool, but there are some rules and regulations that are important to understand. You have to think of the information superhighway as a highway with no traffic laws. But certain rules must be followed or else you may anger your fellow drivers, and you could crash if you don't look where you're going. It's a bit of a strong comparison but it's accurate in many ways.

E-mail is simply electronic mail, sent through what is called your "mail server," which sends your e-mail to the recipient's own mail server and then to the recipient. E-mail addresses read like this: *rob@the-playground.com*. The first part of the e-mail address here is "rob." It identifies the specific user. *@the-playground.com* is the domain where "rob" has his e-mail address. With e-mail, you also have the capability of "attaching" files, perhaps images or just Word or Excel documents, to the e-mail, so the recipient can open them when they receive your e-mail.

Netiquette

Just as there is driving etiquette on the roads, there is Internet etiquette, termed "Netiquette." Practicing Netiquette saves everyone a lot of time and makes the Internet a more manageable place to communicate with other users. The basic rule is to treat online users with the same respect you would a person you know personally. Just because all these users are just text on a screen doesn't mean they're not people, too. Be nice. Simple enough rule, don't you think?

A Web page that acts as an excellent guide to the rules of Netiquette is the Netiquette Home Page, at *http://www.albion .com/netiquette/index.html* (see Figure 4–1).

This page is based on the book *Netiquette* by Virginia Shea. It contains a short summary of the book's message as well a complete online edition of the book. Published in 1994, the book

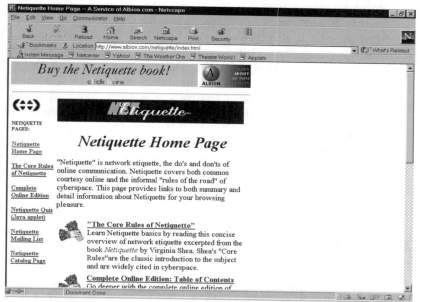

Figure 4–1

inspired reviewers to label Shea as the Ms. Manners of the Internet. Much of what she has to say is extremely valid and much of what she has laid forth is followed to this day. Probably one of the reasons her rules of Netiquette have been so widely embraced is that the book was published just before Internet usage exploded.

When it comes to breaking the rules, one of the most nefarious crimes on the Internet is spamming. Actors in the Chicago area where I live are particularly adept at spamming. E-mailing everyone you know with one message to promote your show is considered bad Netiquette. This is especially true if others pick up the mailing list. Most e-mail programs allow you to "reply" to the sender or to the sender and all other recipients. Therefore, if you send an e-mail to a bunch of your actor friends as well as personal friends, the likely result will be that your personal friends will experience a flurry of e-mails promoting shows that they couldn't care less about. Or they may receive e-mails announcing that someone is going to appear in a national commercial. Bad, bad, bad.

Other no-no's:

- all CAPS: Never use all CAPS. Using all CAPS in e-mails and message boards is equivalent to shouting. Don't shout.
- flaming: Flaming is basically an e-mail or posting of such strong opinion that others will take offense. This practice can result in "flame wars" that can really waste space in newsgroups. If you want to verbally spar with someone, do it away from the public forum.
- reprinting messages. When you hit "reply" to messages, most e-mail and news programs then reprint the text of the message you're replying to. It's considered rude to post a message with the entire text of the message preceding yours. The fact that your subject begins with "Re:" does more than enough to alert the reader that you're replying to a given message. Leaving unnecessary text in a message also increases download time. Simply reprinting text that's one hundred words long may not seem like much, but if everyone did that in a busy newsgroup, it would add up.

Message Boards and Newsgroups

The Internet has many different public forums. The newest form of forum exists on the World Wide Web in message boards and

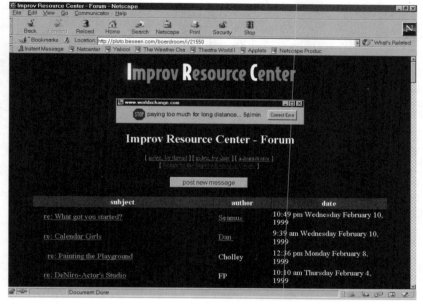

Figure 4–2

live chat rooms (see Figure 4–2). These can be found on newer Web browsers such as the more recent versions of Netscape and Internet Explorer. Live chat rooms, however, are often empty and quiet unless there's a scheduled appearance by someone that ends up inciting an interesting discussion.

An example of a Web-based message board exists at *http://www.sitepowerup.com/mb/view.asp?BoardID=102196*. This is part of a Chicago-based improv page that serves the performers of the city of that particular art form. The Webmaster basically co-ops the service of another Web page in exchange, essentially, for advertising. There are all kinds of these services available. This particular message board is pretty active and sometimes there are people who have interesting things to say.

Usenet is a part of the Internet not nearly as hyped as the Web, because it has no flashy graphics to offer. Usenet is simply an enormous database of "newsgroups" that deal with separate subjects. You can subscribe to any number of these newsgroups, download messages, and reply directly to the sender or post replies to the message board for other subscribers to see.

Depending on the newsreader you use, you will most likely have to download the names of every newsgroup that your ISP makes available to you. This numbers in the thousands but you only have to download the names of the newsgroups once. Periodically, your newsreader will ask you if you would like to see the list of new newsgroups that have emerged since you last used the program. You can set the program up so it doesn't ask you this question, but who knows? A new newsgroup may pop up that fits a subject area that interests you.

When searching for newsgroups to subscribe to, you want to keep your search as short and sweet as possible. Again, if you have a good newsreader like Outlook Express you'll be able to search Usenet for newsgroups with keywords. For example, you can enter "Kubrick" to find out if there is a newsgroup that discusses the films of Stanley Kubrick, and voila! You'll see there *is* one.

The name of the newsgroup, will look something like "alt.movies.kubrick." Each specific word in the name of a newsgroup further defines the subject of a newsgroup. This is important to consider as another part of Netiquette. It is very rude and a waste of space to introduce something in discussion that's off-topic. The first word in the name of the newsgroup defines the broad topic, for example, "alt" for alternative. Companies and universities, for example, can also exist as the first portion of a newsgroup name. There are "utexas" newsgroups and "microsoft" newsgroups, for example.

When you search for newsgroups and find one with a name that might fit your interests you should choose the option to subscribe to it. This subscription is not something you pay for, nor does it mean that the contents of the newsgroup are automatically delivered to you now that you subscribe. All it means is that the list of newsgroups in your software is confined to only those newsgroups you choose to list. Subscriptions save a lot of space and time.

Depending on the volume of the newsgroup, you'll probably want to check for new messages every day. A newsgroup like "rec.arts.theatre.stagecraft" has more than three hundred messages posted a week and it's very time-consuming sifting through so many messages to find something of interest. You have the option of setting your newsreader to download the contents of every unread message so you can scroll through the subject headings while you're offline, but this is only recommended if you have plenty of disk space and the group is not littered with people posting graphics that take time to download. That's yet another rule of netiquette, by the way. If you're going to post to a message board, never post a graphic or a large file unless you're in a newsgroup that specifically states that it is a graphics news-group where people trade pictures.

DEJA NEWS
http://www.dejanews.com

Another option when you're interested in surfing the world of Usenet is a Web site that collects messages from the thousands of newsgroups available and presents them in an easy-to-read fashion.

Deja News separates newsgroups into "channels" of subjects so you won't get confused by all the "alts" and "recs" that I mention above. At the top of the home page, there's a place where you can search for particular keywords in the contents of the thousands of messages passing through Usenet every hour.

Below that is a clever feature that encapsulates random quotes that link to subject threads, which are series of messages posted in reply to the same subject matter. For example, one time when I checked out Deja News there was a quote from someone who posted the following message about a recent Michael Keaton movie: "It's the most moving film I've seen since *Schindler's List.*" Anyone curious as to who would say something so obviously odd could click on the quote and it would send him or her to the related discussion.

Below all that on the home page is the list of channels. They're separated logically and it actually looks like a listing of subjects on a directory like Yahoo!, which I explain more in-depth in the next chapter.

You can also search the archives of particular newsgroups. Since keeping messages on the server for you to access forever would be a waste of space and impossible to muddle through, news servers erase messages after they've been available for a few days or a week. With Deja News, however, you can access the archives of the newsgroups in a search for specific topics. Since messages are otherwise only available for a week or so in normal newsreading software, this could very well be the best feature that Deja News has to offer and certainly is invaluable if you're trying to research a certain topic.

It's an easy page to use and if you are in the position of only having access to a Web browser and no newsreader, it's the best way to get into the world of Usenet.

Now that you know how to reach Usenet, you have to figure out where you're going to trade ideas with fellow human beings, and fellow actors, too. Finding a newsgroup that fits you is a bit of a challenge, but not overwhelmingly so. Sometimes you'll subscribe to a newsgroup because the name looks like something you'd be interested in, but there are no messages. This may be because there is another newsgroup with a similar subject, and over time everyone has chosen to post to that newsgroup instead. There are a lot of redundancies in newsgroup subjects so it requires a little searching to find out where everyone is. Fortunately, unsubscribing to a newsgroup is just as easy as subscribing to one.

To save you some time, I'll go through some of the newsgroups that have discussions that may fit you. Newsgroups are a great way to get questions answered fairly quickly from different sources.

"REC.ARTS.THEATRE.MISC"

This is a place where you can post messages and questions regarding theatre that don't fit into specific categories. You're not going to find postings that just deal with stagecraft or scripts in this newsgroup. An example of one message I saw that was posted in January 1999 was from someone simply asking where one can obtain a script to *The Normal Heart*. There are quite a few people posting messages looking for particular theatre-related Web sites, for example.

When you post a message, again you want to avoid posting just to advertise a show. This newsgroup in particular would be an unfortunate place to start doing that. People who look for newsgroups are often looking for resources.

"REC.ARTS.THEATRE.STAGECRAFT," "ALT.STAGECRAFT," AND "NET.THEATRE.STAGECRAFT"

These three newsgroups deal with stagecraft. For some reason, "rec.arts.theatre.stagecraft" has many more messages posted than "alt.stagecraft." When I looked at each of these newsgroups, there were three hundred messages posted on the former while there were just thirty-four on the latter. There were zero messages posted on "net.theatre.stagecraft," so you might as well not bother subscribing to that newsgroup.

You can post messages inquiring about all kinds of stagecraft problems on these newsgroups. There's also a lot to learn by reading these kinds of newsgroups. Experts often float around these groups offering advice on the best equipment to use. One unsolicited posting, for example, detailed why the writer thought the best CAD program around was MiniCAD. Whether or not you're familiar with everything discussed on a newsgroup, it's still a wonderful reference guide.

"ALT.COMEDY.IMPROVISATION"

This is the newsgroup to check when you're involved in improvisation. Most of the postings are from ComedySportz and TheatreSports performers around the country. Both of these organizations have shows that are usually dedicated to simple improv games. Performers from Chicago, the cradle of improvisation, almost never post to this newsgroup, so if you're a serious student at one of the Chicago institutions or an improv student at a college, it's likely that there really won't be a lot of good information available for you in terms of learning the art of improvisation.

But if you're in the administrative area of forming improv groups, this is a good place for information. There are definitely a few regulars in this group and it's more of a community center where barbs are traded. That's not a bad thing. The Internet is a great place to meet people around the world who have similar interests, and this newsgroup is a particular example of that kind of atmosphere.

"REC.ARTS.THEATRE.PLAYS"

This newsgroup is intended to be a discussion of plays. There's quite a bit of volume on this site. A lot of people post to this newsgroup so your questions could very well be answered. You can ask questions about where to buy plays, whether anyone has ever done a production of play you're considering, or whether a specific play has any good monologues.

The question about *The Normal Heart* that I found in the "rec.arts.theatre.misc" newsgroup might be better suited for this newsgroup. Make sure to ask questions in appropriate newsgroups.

There are quite a few posts advertising an upcoming production of a play, but you really don't want to do that. People from around the world have access to this newsgroup. Who cares if you're opening a production of *Who's Afraid of Virginia Woolf?* in Athens, Ohio? It's a waste of space, honestly, and when you download all the subject headings on any given day you don't want to have to scroll through a bunch of advertisements.

5 Search Engines and Directories

Next there's the Web. The Web has become the great shopping mall of the Internet, with hundreds of millions of pages floating around in cyberspace. The first time you connect to the Web, your browser will most likely have a default home page. This is simply the first Web page that opens at the moment you open your Web browser. Netscape, for example has Netscape Netcenter, *http://www.netscape.com*, which is supposed to act as a good starting-off point for your journey through the Web.

Now that you're connected you have to figure out where you're going. There is no TV Guide-type magazine to tell you what's on the Net. If there were, it wouldn't fit inside your house. If you have trouble keeping track of all the different cable television networks, then keeping track of Web pages is surely your idea of a living hell.

Thus, because of the teeming masses of Web sites out there, surfing is an enormously time-consuming task. If you aimlessly wander the Web, you'll find hours go by before you realize it. This practice is not recommended for anyone who works for a living. You could develop a case of "Internet Addiction." There's even a site that explains what Internet addiction is and how you can tell if you've caught it: *http://www.netaddiction.com*. Thus, you want to make your experience on the Internet as easy and brief as possible.

The best way to explore the Web is to have a pretty good idea of where you want to go. Sometimes you don't have to do much thinking in order to reach a site. When you know you want to visit the NBC Web site, it's a pretty sure bet that the URL is going to be *http://www.nbc.com*. A company that big is going to have its own domain name. The domain name is simply the word that you type before the domain-name extension to tell the browser where you're going. Domain-name extensions include

.com: U.S. commercial sites
.org: U.S. nonprofit sites (like Web sites for museums)
.gov: U.S. federal government Web sites
.edu: educational institute Web pages

The list goes on. There are more domain-name extensions for Web sites that originate in a specific country. While a site like NBC or ESPN will have an obvious URL, millions and millions of other Web sites have long URLs because they don't have their own domain names or someone else already reserved the domain name they wanted. Thus, some pages might have a URL that looks similar to this: *http://www.enteract.com/~hatsoff/dougandmary*.

That's actually one of my Web pages. The domain name is simply the domain name of my ISP. The little "~" before "hatsoff" is a tilda. This designates the Web page as a page of the user "hatsoff" underneath the banner of the Enteract service. Everything after "~hatsoff" is designated by the user. Thus, my Douglas Fairbanks and Mary Pickford page is contained inside the folder "dougandmary."

As you can tell, it's pretty hard to simply guess what the URL is in this case. Many Web sites have a URL similar to that one, and that's when you have to rely on search tools to find Web sites that fit the subject area you're interested in.

There are two search tools that can help you: directories and search engines. Directories are Web sites that are built by humans and allow you to search through their humanmade databases to find Web sites that fit your search parameters. Search engines are Web sites that use software to detect your search words in millions of Web sites and then give you hyperlinks to sites that they believe best fit your want.

Directories

YAHOO!
http://www.yahoo.com

Yahoo! is the world's most famous directory and also happens to be the most visited site on the Web. It was created in April 1994 at Stanford University by David Filo and Jerry Yang as a way to keep track of their personal interests on the Internet. During the course of that year they converted it into a customized database for the thousands of users that had begun to use Yahoo! Yahoo! stands for "Yet Another Hierarchical Officious Oracle." It has grown in its short life into a powerful company with millions of dollars of advertising revenue and millions of "hits"—viewings— a day and television commercials during NFL games on Sundays.

When you visit the Yahoo! Web site, you'll see a page with dozens and dozens of hyperlinks. It can be overwhelming, especially if it's the first web site you've ever encountered, but it's fairly simple really. Near the top of the home page is a space where you can enter a word or words that fit what you're looking for. For example, when I entered "acting" into the space provided, the rsearch returned with seventeen hyperlinks of categories. Yahoo! is split up into hundreds and hundreds of categories, subcategories, and sub-subcategories that come closer and closer to what you're looking for.

I also received 242 site matches that had the word *acting* in their descriptions. When Webmasters submit their site for inclusion on Yahoo!, they offer a short description of their site along with the name and URL. They also get to choose what category they want the site to fall under. Since Yahoo! gets so many thousands of submissions, it takes a week or two to get approval, but then the URL is up under the category the Webmaster chose. The disadvantage of finding Web sites on Yahoo! is that the directory only includes the sites that have been submitted and approved.

If you want to use a search word that contains more than one word, you must remember to put quotation marks around the entire phrase, for example, "hot dog." If you don't include those quotes, Yahoo! will search for all Web sites that feature either the word *hot* or the word *dog* without any concern as to whether the words appear together in their culinary context. And in general, you want to be as specific as possible with search words, without being *too* specific. For example, it might not be the best idea to enter "Like a Rolling Stone" when you want to look for web sites about Bob Dylan. You should probably enter "Bob Dylan" in this case.

Besides being the most popular directory on the Web, Yahoo! features so many things now that it has become like a community center on the Web, with free e-mail as well as a search capability for e-mail addresses and phone numbers. Yahoo! Maps lets you enter a specific address and then shows you a map of the surrounding area and can also give you driving directions to any location you desire.

There are other directories out there, but they do not have the scope and power that Yahoo! does. Still, it's always good to cover all your bases and use more than one search whenever you're looking for multiple sites under the banner of one subject area. Since directories are built by humans, none of them is perfect or includes every Web site that exists. Since Yahoo! is the largest directory in the world, it takes a lot longer for a Web site to be included than it might a smaller directory. Thus, the newer the Web site, the more likely it will be included in a smaller directory rather than Yahoo!

LOOK SMART
http://www.looksmart.com

This directory labels itself as "the next generation user-oriented navigation service." There are two search options available. You can search the Web or search "your town." When you enter the city you're closest to the directory supplies the current weather as well as links and an entertainment guide. For more powerful searches, Look Smart utilizes the AltaVista search engine.

MAGELLAN INTERNET GUIDE
http://magellan.excite.com

This directory is owned by Excite, which is a search engine. It has a very uncluttered home page, which may appeal to those who find Yahoo!'s a jumbled mess. Magellan is different from other directories in that it provides short reviews of the Web sites that result when you enter a search.

WEBCRAWLER
http://www.webcrawler.com

This veteran directory is also owned by Excite. It's set up much like Yahoo! and if you enter a search parameter that exceeds the capability of the existing directory it will search on Excite.

SNAP
http://www.snap.com

Snap is owned by Cnet and is another directory that is intended to be a starting-off point, like a community center for the Web.

And while there are other directories out there, this should provide you with more than a good starting point. Now I'll describe a few search engines. They differ from directories in that the search results are compiled by software rather than.

Search Engines

Search engines' results come about from software made up of "spiders." I'm not kidding. Spiders detect Web sites automatically, based on the search words you enter. Thus, if you were to enter "monologue" the search engine would send its spider along millions of Web sites it has detected in the past and search for the word *monologue*. As you might expect, thousands of hyperlinks usually come up that fit your search parameter, no matter which search engine you choose to use. After all, the spiders do not discriminate between pages that are actually about monologues and those pages that simply contain the word *monologue* somewhere in their texts. Almost all search engines order the hyperlinks by the consistent recurrence of the word or words you list, but search engines are powerful tools and you have to learn how to use them properly or else you'll wind up sifting through ninety-six hundred hyperlinks in order to find a site with monologues for actors.

When you decide, for example, that you're going to search for monologues, you should think about what you *don't* want. Some search engines employ Boolean logic, which refers to a system of logical thought pioneered by George Boole (1815–64), which is based on the idea of "AND" and "OR" as operators for searches. When you enter "monologues AND Jay Leno," for example, the search engine will search for Web sites that contain both words. When they enter "monologues OR Jay Leno," as you can imagine, it will search for Web sites that contain either one of the words.

Another option is to type "monologues NOT Jay Leno" in order to exclude any Web sites that mention the words *monologue* and *Jay Leno*. This process of elimination procedure is useful. When you simply enter "monologue," you'll notice Web sites that mention they have copies of late-night talk-show monologues. As an actor, you're really not interested in that claptrap. So you want to slim down your search parameters as much as possible.

Also, you want to be careful when you enter the words "theatre" or "theatre" in a search. You want to include both, simply because different Webmasters around the world are going to spell it differently. Search engines are not going to guess what the Webmasters mean by how they spell theatre. They search for specific words exactly as you spell them, so it's smart to type "theatre OR theatre" in your search request.

Judging from the appearance of search engines, you'd probably think they're all the same. But when you're making searches, you'll want to keep in mind the accuracy of the results, how easy it is to make searches and how advanced the searches can get on a particular search engine. "Advanced" means getting your searches as specific as possible.

I entered the term "silent films" in each of the following search engines to test them out. If you want to know more about your search engine choices, CNET's Review of Search Engines at *http://www.cnet.com/Content/Reviews/Compare/Search2/?st.cn. fd.accol.re* is an excellent place to look. CNet is a wonderful source for just about any information on the Web. Among the topics it covers are reviews of software, Web sites, and everything else under the sun. The above URL takes you to a series of of Web site reviews that is much more detailed than the ones below.

EXCITE

http://www.excite.com

Excite's home page is a crowded treasure trove of information. Stocks information appears to the left. News headlines accompany search subjects. As a default page for your Web browser, it's really second to none. It's a fantastic place to start your journey on the Web in a little community center.

Entering "silent films" got me 1,670 results, and no, I didn't look through them all. Next to each link, Excite put a percentage of certainty that it fit my request, and the highest confidence it had was 76 percent, although many sites dealt with silent films. CNet's review section complains of too many out-of-date links and duplicate links in Excite's searches.

HOTBOT

http://www.hotbot.com

It's hard to miss this page with its fluorescent colors. CNet voted it best search engine. I got 2,640 matches for "silent films" with quite a few sites that were on the mark. HotBot also lists percentage of certainty for each result, and its highest was 99 percent for pages that definitely had something to do with silent films.

ALTAVISTA
http://www.altavista.com

When I entered "silent films" here, more than thirty-nine hundred results came back. I've often searched on AltaVista and it's so incredibly comprehensive that it's really hard to find exactly what you're looking for. But if comprehensive is what you're looking for, Alta Vista is probably your best bet.

GO
http://www.go.com

Formerly known as Infoseek and bought by the Go network, Go is set up much like Excite and Yahoo! with news headlines as well as categories for searches, giving you a good starting page for your Web browser (see Figure 5–1). When I entered "silent films" on this search engine, I got an overwhelming 6,135 results. Go also lists links in order of certainty and the most certain percentage was 77 percent. Most pages dealt with the subject. This page was CNet's second favorite search engine behind Hotbot.

The more specific and specialized your search needs are, the more important it is to use a comprehensive search such as AltaVista.

There's one more category to go through: meta-search engines.

Meta-Search Engines

Meta-search engines are Web sites that search all of the big search engines simultaneously and give you a consolidated report of the results. It's a great way to get a lot of research done in one lump sum.

ASK JEEVES
http://www.askjeeves.com

Ask Jeeves is a meta-search engine that promises "Smart answers fast!" It's cleverly disguised as a sort of "answer-man" page, in

Figure 5–1: Reprinted by permission. Infoseek, Ultrasmart, Ultraseek, Ultraseek Server, Infoseek Desktop, Infoseek Ultra, iSeek, Quickseek, Imageseek, Ultrashop, the Infoseek logos, and the tagline "Once you know, you know" are trademarks of Infoseek Corporation which may be registered in certain jurisidictions. Other trademarks shown are trademarks of their respective owners. Copyright © 1994–1999 Infoseek Corporation. All rights reserved.

which you simply ask a question like "Where can I buy scrims?" It then returns a list of questions that come close to your question with buttons next to them to take you to a page that may very well answer your question. The meta-search engine powering Ask Jeeves will go through the engines of Excite, Infoseek, etc., as well as directories like Yahoo! and come up with a list of responses, even going so far as to point out where it got its answers.

When I entered the question, "Where can I buy scrims?" the following questions appeared:

"Where can I buy arts and crafts online?"
"Where can I find financial advice?"
"Where can I find information on how to buy beanie babies?"

OK, not perfect. However, following those questions are more links to pages that come close to what you want, each found through the various search engines and directories, making Ask Jeeves a nice one-stop search shop.

METACRAWLER
http://www.metacrawler.com

Metacrawler uses several search engines to conduct its searches. It's laid out like a normal search engine. The cool part is on the home page. There's a long column on the left-hand side of the window called "The Marketplace" that features links to Outpost.com, travel sites, and other commerce sites. It makes quick searches very easy, and the front page isn't as "busy" as many of the other sites out there.

DOGPILE
http://www.dogpile.com

Dogpile is a more simple-looking page, but it packs a punch, using just about every major search engine there is. The only drawback is that it doesn't eliminate duplicate links from separate search engines.

Overall, when using at search engines, directories, and meta-search engines, you might still have problems finding what you're looking for. In that case, you might have to accept the idea that out of 340 million Web pages, there isn't one that has exactly what you're looking for.

But because there are so many Web pages, there are often talented Webmasters who do the searching for you within your particular subject area and give you the chance to link to many other sites that interest actors. Many Web sites have "Links" pages built in that contain links to Web sites that are relevant to those interested in the subject matter of the site they're visiting at the moment. This is often how surfing begins.

Next, I'm going to describe some pages that exist as resources for actors, both as informational tools and as platforms from which you can crawl the Web for other sites for actors.

Education 6

B efore you act, you have to learn how. The Internet provides by far the best resource for researching the countless learning centers around the world that will allow you to explore every facet of the acting experience.

When you're looking for places to learn, you can use the search engines and directories to narrow your searches by location, acting style and type of school. I'm going to tell you a little bit what's out there. Obviously, it would be impossible to include an exhaustive list of Web sites covering every acting school in the world in this book But I'll introduce you to some of the Web sites you can take a gander at in your noble quest to become the greatest actor since whoever you think the greatest actor is.

First, I'll tell you about some guides to colleges and universities. These are specialized directories that will get you to your desired destination a lot faster than a huge general directory like Yahoo! that covers every subject on the planet. These sites are specifically designed for you.

Since colleges and universities have so much manpower and are often large and powerful, nearly every college and university in the country maintains at least a modest presence on the Web. The Internet is a wonderful tool to send potential students all kinds of information about their institutions. Remember the days when you had to go to college fairs and nearly separate your shoulders carrying plastic bags full of propaganda brochures? Now those brochures are online! And while few of the Web sites will ever knock your socks off with graphics or Java applets or animations, they usually do a good job of providing basic information on the schools, which is all that really matters in this context.

When searching for colleges and universities, and acting training centers, for that matter, you want to start out with a broad scope, perhaps with searches based on location. The following sites can provide you with the resources to start your quest.

OVERVIEW OF COLLEGES, VOCATIONAL SCHOOLS AND CAREERS
AND OVERVIEW OF COLLEGE FINANCIAL AID
http://www.overview.com/colleges/index.html and
http://www.overview.com/colleges/college-financial-aid.htm

The sort of specialized directory found on these sites is a good place to start. You have many search parameters. Under "Career Field" you'll want to choose *Visual and Performing Arts*, and after you choose that there will be more specific criteria you can enter, whether it covers film, writing, or performance.

It's important to understand that sites like these are not totally comprehensive and you shouldn't depend on them entirely. For example, my own search for schools with acting and directing programs with a tuition of more than $10,000 in the state of Illinois only brought back one result: DePaul University. Now, everyone and his cousin in the state of Illinois knows that Northwestern University fits all the criteria of my search and yet it is curiously omitted.

These sites also features a page of links to pages that can help you find financial aid.

COLLEGE AND UNIVERSITY HOME PAGES—ALPHABETICAL LISTING
http://www.mit.edu/people/cdemello/univ.html

When you first enter this site, you'll notice that it appears to be just a boring mass of text. However, don't let the lack of graphics and gimmicks fool you into thinking this site has no content. You may also believe this site is horribly out of date, since according to the home page, it hasn't been updated since 1996.

Quite the contrary, this page is a gloriously detailed list of links to college and university home pages from around the world. As you can guess from the title of the page, the list is alphabetical. Thus, you need to know which specific school or schools you're looking for, but it's still a very comprehensive and useful site that you should bookmark and browse frequently in your search for an education.

You also have the option of searching through schools based on geography rather than the alphabet.

EMBARK.COM (FORMERLY COLLEGEEDGE) AND COLLEGENET
http://www.embark.com and http://www.collegenet.com

These two sites are ambitious guides to undergraduate and graduate programs and include online applications for participating schools.

CollegeNET is a Web site put together by a company called Universal Algorithms, which provides "workflow enhancement solutions" to colleges and universities. It was launched in February 1995 and is partnered with more than 190 colleges and universities to provide online applications.

The home page is a black screen with stars (a starfield) with a simple graphic pointing you to the different components of the site:

- College Search: On this page you simply enter the search criteria you want, from price of tuition to majors. The first page of the college search allows you to narrow down to four-year schools, vocational schools, or grad schools, becoming even more specific to MBA programs and medical schools.
- CollegeBOT Crawler: This page has its own unique URL at *http://www.collegebot.com* and touts itself as the only search engine that looks through education-related sites.
- Financial Aid and Scholarships: This page is a simple series of links to various sources of information. CollegeNET itself has a scholarship that you're automatically eligible for if you go through the online application process.
- College Recruiting "Standout": This page tells you about CollegeNET's service that enables you to become visible to the 150—and allegedly growing—colleges and universities that use the CollegeNET database so they can seek you out and recruit you even if you haven't submitted an application. According to the page, enrollment in this program is $9.

The site attempts to be the definitive source of information about all subjects dealing with the process of getting into an institution of higher learning, as does Embark.com.

Embark.com is run by a company called Snap Technologies, which was founded in the summer of 1995 by five friends who had grown up in the information technology industry. Having gone to public high schools that offered little guidance in the process of choosing a college, they decided to create Embark.com to fill the gap on the Internet for this kind of service.

The Embark.com homepage is split into sections for admissions professionals and guidance professionals, as well as students who are interested in either undergraduate or graduate programs. The home page allows you to be even more specific to begin with by providing a link right there for MBA and law programs. But you don't care about that—you're an actor!

There are participating schools for which you can apply online. The Embark.com recruiter is a similar program to CollegeNET's Standout. They also offer a SNAP/Embark.com scholarship.

COLLEGE VIEW
http://www.collegeview.com

This site offers all kinds of information on colleges and even has a search function that, unfortunately, failed to work each time I attempted to use it. However, even without that function, the site is useful for its series of articles on choosing a career, which, as a reader of a book for actors, you probably have done already, and other topics like financial aid.

COLLEGE NIGHT
http://www.collegenight.com

When I came upon the home page of this site I was rather put out by how much the site hypes itself. It's kind of like television advertsiements that plug the program you're currently watching. Why advertise something I'm in the process of using at that moment? Worse than that, in order to enter the site, you have to enter your e-mail address. As a frequent recipient of junk e-mail, I don't like to submit my e-mail address anywhere.

Still, once entering the site, you really have a load of information and links thrust at you in a simple, pleasant way. It's a great way to get to Web pages that deal with college entrance exams like the SAT and ACT, as well as other links that help you get to the college you're looking for.

COLLEGE IS POSSIBLE
http://www.collegeispossible.com

This attractive site is mostly a guide for parents who need to make long-term plans to send their children to college. However, there is useful information on financial aid programs and a resource library of links to relevant pages.

COLLEGE BOARD ONLINE
http://www.collegeboard.org

The College Board is that wonderful organization that brings you such epic tests as the SAT. Its Web site is very large. On the home page, you're given a menu of options for starting points on the site. The top selection is "Starting Points for Students and Parents." After clicking on that menu item, you get to a page with yet more links to other pages.

One link takes you to a whole list of financial aid options. Another series of links helps you plan ahead with your career choice. Another list of links is called "Getting Ready for the Tests" which we lucky ones have passed by long ago.

There are also pages designed to help you look for a college, such as the following one.

College Search
http://cbweb1.collegeboard.org/csearch/

This portion of the College Board Web site is a simple search tool. When I first took a look at this page, it was painfully slow to come back with the next page of search criteria after I had clicked on the "Submit" button, even with my fast modem. Also, if you have one hundred or more results from your search, the site doesn't show the results at all, forcing you to tighten your search parameters.

However, once you have entered all your search criteria, a list of colleges appears and you can get information about said college on a Web page that you can print out for your records. The page lists admission deadlines and requirements as well as addresses and phone numbers. The major flaw is a lack of a link to that college's Web page. Still, this is an invaluable resource if you're looking for admission information, including various requirements and deadlines.

VIRTUAL CAMPUS TOURS
http://www.campustours.com

This very cool site links to various virtual campus tours with different colleges and universities. You can search by location or alphabet and the site will give you a grid of schools with links to the home pages of the schools. The site offers links to virtual tours, which are basically the online versions of propaganda pamphlets but they are very useful and quick ways to get an overview of a schools. The site offers links to Webcams, although the majority of schools don't have them. A Webcam is a still picture of a campus as it looks at the instant you load the Web page. It offers little else than a picture but at least you get to see whether the campus looks like it's supposed to look.

Also, those schools that have online video available have links on Campus Tours, as well as interactive maps. This site is probably the best of the college search pages, and it's also updated frequently. It's a great place to search for colleges that suit your needs.

GRADSCHOOLS.COM
http://www.gradschools.com

Now when it comes to those of you who already have your undergraduate degrees, this site is a wonderful search tool for grad schools. Like a lot of the sites outlined above, it gives you the option to search by subject area and then by geographic location. When results come back, they are accompanied by buttons that allow you to e-mail those schools for more information.

GRADUATE SCHOOL GUIDE ONLINE
http://www.schoolguides.com

This site is identical in purpose to the site above but gives you another source of information so you don't have to pigeonhole yourself into just receiving a flow of data from one place. It's just as effective a tool, and it also gives you search criteria by major and location.

Financial Aid

When making the general search for colleges and universities, you must concern yourself with how much the school is going to cost. No matter the area of study you want to pursue, financial aid is extremely important. The following Web sites will assist you in figuring out the best way to pay for a college education.

FINAID
http://www.finaid.org

This page is really the best place to look for financial aid information. It is the most comprehensive guide to a single subject I've ever seen, offering what seems to be as many links as a directory like Yahoo! to any number of subjects dealing with financial aid. There are links to tools that help you calculate your financial aid needs, links to specific school financial aid pages, links to actual government Web sites that tell you about federal aid and any number of links to any number of pages. Not only that, it offers a comprehensive list of links to databases of every scholarship imaginable!

MOLIS SCHOLARSHIP SEARCH
http://www.fie.com/molis/scholar.htm

This site is an excellent search tool for scholarships for only *minority* applicants. Search criteria are well laid out. You have the options of entering ethnicity, nation of origin, GPA, and state in which you currently reside to receive a list of potential scholarships, each linked to its own page with complete information so you can find out if it's worth the effort to apply for said scholarship.

KAPLOAN
http://www1.kaplan.com/view/zine/

This online 'zine has a lot of good information on paying for both college and graduate schools. There is information on just about every form of student loan and scholarship available and although it is slow, it still has very detailed and crucial information that you will need if you want to pay for school.

Online Training

As much as you rely on the actual process of acting and exercises you also should read the advice and wisdom of those who have gone before you. There are a few Web sites that offer actual text that gives insight into the training and preparation of an actor. I wish there were more. The best example of online training comes in the form of a journal from Chicago, Illinois, written by Second City Mainstage director Mick Napier, called the Paradigm Lost Journal.

THE PARADIGM LOST JOURNAL
http://www.annoyance.com/mainstage.html

This Web site is run by a Chicago-based theatre company that offers training in improvisation. What sets it apart from other Web sites regardless of the content of the shows on stage is an amazing feature called "The Paradigm Lost Journal." This journal is one of the best things I've seen on the Web in a stage-related capacity and it's a shame that more teachers don't offer this kind of feature on their Web pages.

Mick Napier, who is the founder of the Annoyance Theatre, has directed several revues on the Second City main stage in Chicago. If you're not familiar with Second City revues, they are simply revues with various comedy sketches, songs, and the like. The shows are written almost entirely from improvisation in rehearsals.

At the beginning of 1997, while preparing to put up the new Second City revue that eventually became "Paradigm Lost," Napier decided to write about the process of creating the show on his Annoyance Theatre page. In diary entries that fully revealed the joy and rage of putting any kind of production together, Napier informs and entertains.

The following is an excerpt from the journal dated January 20, 1997:

> All in all, the skits are fine. The show is holding up well. All new material that held up pretty good over the weekend. Still too many 2 person scenes, too much sitting, and toooooooooo conventional Second City. Worried? Not a fucking bit. We have ample time, a great cast, good material on the boards, and I completely trust myself.
>
> This makes me think of something. The other night an

alumnus of Second City was watching the show. And what I
noticed is that I was not watching him. Now what does that
mean? That means that it occurred to me that I didn't care
what he thought. I respect him well enough and he's a good
guy and he's directed before, etc. . . . but I just don't care
what other people think at this point. It used to be that I
would watch the producer or another actor or director or
anyone else I respected to check out their reaction. Now I
just don't . . . such a waste of time, and it's all because I trust
myself. Now that doesn't mean that I won't accept suggestions or opinions. . . ."

This kind of spontaneous writing is what the Internet can
offer if used correctly. Another excerpt shows more about
what Napier could offer for students of improvisation by writing this journal entry, dated December 10, 1996:

Context

What does the audience need to know? An audience needs a
context to follow in every scene. If the audience doesn't
know the roadmap, they won't understand, they can't enjoy
the game. Dorothy must stay in Oz, and have the single
desire to go back to Kansas. Lots of shit can go down in Oz,
but she must stay there and try everything to get home. The
second she gets back to Kansas, that scene is over. If while
in Oz, she decides she likes it there and wants to stay, she
violates the integrity of the context she declared. I believe
one must always look at the quality of context in a scene. If
we think it's funny but the audience doesn't, what contextual
decision can we make to invite the audience in. Sometimes
it's the least little thing . . . a line, a word, a sound, a physi-
cal move. The scene can be as absurd as you'd like, but have
your context shit intact or you will alienate your audience . . .
which is a context in and of itself.

Having been involved in the improvisational theatre community
in Chicago for five years, I was struck most by the fact that everyone who was on the Internet read the journal. Jason Chin, director of the Training Center at ImprovOlympic commented,

I was reading the on-line journal while Mick was in the
process of directing the show and I was working the sou-
venir booth at Second City. It was amazing. I would watch
the improv sets and then read the update the very next day.
Absolutely fascinating stuff. The very first public attempt to

capture the elusive nature of Second City production. I'm an improv student so watching the scene selection process and the whole evolution of the thing was wonderful. Mick directs and he directs with a passion that is conveyed through the journal. To read it and then watch the work in progress. . . .

The improv community was galvanized. All because of a Web site. Granted, Chicago's theatre community is unique in its self-support—it's the greatest theatre town in the world; did I mention that?—but still, it's a shame more Web pages like this aren't offered.

ACTING WORKSHOP ON-LINE (AWOL)
http://www.execpc.com/~blankda/acting2.html

This is an attempt to provide an online acting school. The best part of the site is as an Amazon.com associate, linking you to Amazon.com pages where you can buy specific books that are supposed to assist you in learning to be an actor. The site also contains little essays that give you a kind of primer course in acting. It also has a page full of links to acting training centers that looks quite full but it not a completely comprehensive list. However, it's a good start. The page is worth looking at.

Acting Schools

If you want to study acting at an institute or school or are you looking for a simple class to brush up on your Meisner, there are really two different categories of acting schools to choose from. There are the intense multiyear programs—often expensive and in New York—and there are the more specialized, inexpensive schools of acting, where you can take six-week courses often concentrating on specific areas of acting, such as Meisner or improvisation.

I'll tell you about some acting schools in different arenas. There isn't enough space here to mention every acting school in the world, so I hope I don't get angry letters for excluding your favorite.

Figure 6–1

ACTING SCHOOLS, COURSES AND TRAINING CLASSES
http://pages.prodigy.net/kenstock/schools.htm

This is a one-page site that offers a few links to acting school and training center home pages. There are also links to theatre schools that make their homes at universities around the country. There are very few links on this site—only about a couple dozen—but it never hurts to take a detailed look at a site even as modest as this, because perhaps it contains a gem that no one else found. It's possible.

TISCH SCHOOL OF THE ARTS
http://www.nyu.edu/tisch

This school is expensive. However, all kinds of interesting people came from NYU's Tisch School of the Arts, for example, Spike Lee. It's a very distinguished school and has become one of the most respected in the world, possibly *the* most respected. Although one cannot judge a school by its cover, the home page is a dazzling collage of animations detailing each of the disciplines taught in the school (see Figure 6–1). There are pages dealing with alumni news, a page of admission requirements, and other "normal" college information. I couldn't find any information on how much it all costs, though!

AMERICAN ACADEMY OF DRAMATIC ARTS
http://www.aada.org

This is another highly respected and decorated school that boasts famous alumni. However, be warned: When I logged onto this Web page, the right frame had no scroll bar on the right, meaning you have to highlight words and drag down in order to scroll down a page. Pretty annoying, if you ask me.

NORTHWESTERN UNIVERSITY SCHOOL OF SPEECH
http://www.nwu.edu/speech/departments/theatre.html

Here's another example of one of the most well-respected theatre schools in the country. Northwestern's Web site isn't nearly as visually striking as Tisch's Web site, but don't let that deter you from checking it out. It still provides you with the information you need to give you a pretty good idea of what the schools offers to the potential actor. Fancy graphics are the least important feature of college Web sites, so make sure you pay attention to the content of these sites instead of only looking at those that have pretty pictures.

STELLA ADLER CONSERVATORY OF ACTING
http://www.stellaadler.com/

This acting school is right in Manhattan's Greenwich Village, which, if you're really serious about the stage, is where you want to be if you ever hope to make any kind of a living at it. That doesn't mean Chicago isn't the greatest theatre town in the world, but there's plenty more money to be made in New York.

The Stella Adler Conservatory is right in the thick of it. The Web site's home page goes right into the life story of the founder of the conservatory, Stella Adler. The site is very simple but gives the necessary information and has a form you can fill out to receive more information about the school's programs.

ACT ONE STUDIOS
http://www.actone.com

This studio is an example of the many places to train in Chicago. This site is again fairly basic, but attractive. Unfortunately, there's no online form to register for classes.

TRIPLE THREAT THEATRE STUDIO
http://www.3threat.com

An example of an acting school in a town that you wouldn't normally consider a haven for actors, the Triple Threat Theatre Studio advertises itself as having "a bold new approach in training for the performing arts." It's located in Kent Island, Maryland. Its selling point is that it teaches actors how to sing, dance, and act all in one training program. Small gems like this are worth looking into if they fit your needs as a performer.

IMPROVOLYMPIC AND IMPROVOLYMPIC WEST
http://www.improvolymp.com and http://www.iowest.com

In Chicago and Los Angeles, Charna Halpern and the late Del Close's unique approach to improvisation as a performance art in itself is practiced and taught at ImprovOlympic. As the only major training center in the world in long-form improvisational theatre, IO as we we call it in Chicago, has a Web site for each of its two locations. Each Web site has its own distinct look and style, reflecting the different personalities running each theatre and training center. The founders still run the show in Chicago, while those students of theirs who have moved on to film and television run the show in L.A. Both Web sites are worth looking at if you're interested in improvisation whether you're in the Midwest or on the West Coast.

And, of course, there are many more sites out there. Refer to Chapter 5 to learn how to find them.

7 *Online Magazines*

One of my personal favorite aspects of the Web is the opportunity to read at least portions of all kinds of magazines and newspapers online instead of having to browse at a bookstore for hours. Online versions of magazines, as well as exclusively online magazines, which are sometimes called Webzines, often give you what you expect from the hard copies of magazines and newspapers, such as feature articles and regular columns, but they also have unique features that you can only get on the Web. If you have a monthly magazine, the Web can supplement it with material that comes at a greater frequency.

I'm going to show you some literary Web sites that offer some useful information for actors. They're not all exclusively for actors, but there are some like *Variety* that, if you live in Los Angeles, or New York especially, are very important reading for anyone in the entertainment community. While I wouldn't suggest every actor in the world to run out and subscribe to something like *Variety,* for example, the Web lets you get at least part of the experience at either no cost or little cost.

PLAYBILL ON-LINE
http://www.playbill.com

This online version of *Playbill* is quite useful. It has a traditional home page, consisting of headlines that function as hyperlinks to the corresponding articles. Along the left side of the home page is a column with links to other portions of the Web site. The headlines featured on the day I checked out the site led to stories on Robert Falls' revival of *Death of a Salesman* opening in New York, news on the second pre-Broadway engagement of Elton John and Tim Rice's *Aida* and news on many other productions opening in New York.

Also featured on the home page is an offer to join Playbill's online club for free. Joining makes you eligible for discount ticket offers as well as dining and travel discount offers. You just have to supply basic geographical information so the site will only send you offers that apply to your area. You can also request that the site not e-mail offers to you.

Your username and password for joining the club also allows you to visit the "members only" portion of the site. This page links you to various special offers. Most of the offers apply to New York, as you might imagine, but they're there.

Back on the home page of this site, in the left column there are links to more news items on theatre both in the United States and abroad. There are links to show listings for Broadway, Off Broadway, Regional, National Tour, London, and Summer Stock. Clicking on a link takes you to a form that allows you to enter more specific information on a listing or listings you'd like to see, narrowing down your search options for theatre name, name of show, etc. The listings are up-to-date and comprehensive.

Along the same left column there's a "mall" where you can buy tickets through Tele-Charge (*http://www.telecharge.com*) and buy books, among other items. There's a link to job postings, for everything from performing to administrative work in the industry. Most job postings are for New York-area jobs, but there are postings for other areas of the country as well so you should look here if you're interested in another option for a job hunt.

Probably my favorite part of this site is the gallery of artwork from theatres and *Playbill* covers as well as production photos. It's a chance to see a diverse group of artists' interpretations of various plays. And, even further down on the left column of the home page is a link to seating charts to various theatres, mostly in New York, and there are links to the Drama Book Shop and Theatre Central, which are covered elsewhere in this book.

Overall, Playbill is one of the very best theatre resource sites on the Internet. It might be *the* best.

BACK STAGE
http://www.backstagecasting.com

This Web site from BPI Electronic Media is a fantastic resource. It's owned by the same folks who run the online versions of *Billboard* and *The Hollywood Reporter*, among other sites. This site is set up as a newspaper would be, with the masthead proclaiming it as "The Complete Online Performing Arts Resource." And it achieves that purpose.

Every day the site is updated and features up-to-the-minute articles and profiles of performing artists of our times. To the immediate left of the masthead in the left column there is a series of links to other resources on the Back Stage site. One such resource is the "Performing Arts Directory." The Performing Arts Directory is a series of scroll-down menus linking you to important sites covering everything from acting coaches to fitness to voice-overs and jingles.

Another link on the left column of the front page is "Casting," which gives you information on casting notices, arranged by region.

There's the "News Index," which provides links to the several news stories the site has reported over the past week or so, divided into sections devoted to New York and Los Angeles.

Another section titled "Aisle Seat" is intended as a guide for audiences, although that's not entirely clear. This is divided into three sections. "Theatre" provides show listings for Broadway, Off Broadway, off Off Broadway, dance, and Los Angeles theatre. There are also reviews of shows. The "Film" section only featured two articles the last time I looked and "Television" featured just one article. Presumably these two sections will expand to feature as much as the "Theatre" section does.

Another link from the front page is "Career Corner." As of this writing, it was a section that promotes itself as "Coming Soon." It's intended to be an all-purpose page for aiding you in your career, with how-to essays and a message board for you to post questions.

"Feature Stories" contains stories on everything from profiles of production teams of the latest HBO productions to a profile on character actor Alfred Molina.

The Web site offers details on the print version of Back Stage as well. Overall it's a great site to browse at least a few times a week just to make sure you're in the know in the entertainment industry.

VARIETY AND THE HOLLYWOOD REPORTER
http://www.variety.com and http://www.hollywoodreporter.com

Variety and *The Hollywood Reporter* are the two newspapers you're supposed to read every day in L.A. if you're an actor. Both papers offer Web sites and Web services exclusively to those who subscribe to the online versions.

While that makes it sound like nonsubscribers won't see anything on either Web site, that's not quite true. Take the *Variety* Web site, for example. Each day the home page of the Web site offers links to the feature articles in *Daily Variety*. This is free to any user. There are also reviews, Army Archerd's column, and articles on the big film fests like Cannes. Subscribers to what they call "Variety Extra" receive the full text of every article in *Daily Variety* the night before the paper hits the streets, as well as a searchable archive of the past year's issues of *Variety*, the box office charts, and more of the regular columns. Subscriptions are $33 a month for those who don't subscribe to the print version and $15 a month for those who do.

The Hollywood Reporter's Web site is structured much the same way. Top stories are included on the free portion of the site, separated into news on film, television, and the international industry. The "Premium" section offers you stories the night before they appear in print, all the production charts, all the archives stretching back to 1992 and what it calls its script-sales feature, which enables you to see which scripts Hollywood is buying. Online subscriptions "cost $14.95 a month. The first 10 full-text displays of news stories, reviews, archived items or production listings are free of additional charges each month. After that, the charge is only 10 cents per current news story or posted review; 25 cents per archived story, review or column; and 25 cents per production listing (to read, print and/or download each file)." There is no discount for people who already subscribe to the print version.

SHAKESPEARE MAGAZINE
http://www.shakespearemag.com

If you are really interested in the Bard, this online version of the magazine is the place to be. While it doesn't feature all the text from the magazine, something which few magazines are likely to do because they make their profits through subscriptions to their magazines, not access to their Web sites, it still features a couple of full articles from the current issue that are labeled "Featured Web articles" as well as synopses of the rest of the articles in the issue.

From the front page you can also link to relevant news, as well as a page of teaching resources. You can access the teaching resources page by entering a password found in the current issue of the magazine. Clever. The resources page features "a collection of dynamic lesson plans for teaching Shakespeare in all kinds of classrooms with all kinds of students." The site adds one lesson plan to the site per issue. There's also an archives page and a "bookshelf" page, which were under construction at the time I accessed the site.

STAGEBILL
http://www.stagebill.com

While Playbill has the "theatre program" industry locked up in New York City, *Stagebill* is the big player in Chicago and some other places too. *Stagebill's* banner headline on its Web site promotes itself as "The Premier Guide to the Performing Arts." The home page is compact, with a search option that gives you pull-down menus to search by region and type of performing art. I chose "Chicago" and "Theatre." You also have the option of choosing any date or "today." I chose today. In some cases, the search results were accurate. The show they had listed at the Goodman Theatre was correct but the show they had listed at Second City was incorrect.

Under a little line drawing of performers on the home page, there are links to "Theatre," "Dance," "Opera," "Jazz," and "Classical." Each link leads you to a page of articles and profiles dealing with each individual subject. The articles are fairly up-to-date and are fairly Chicago-centric.

On each one of these subject pages, there's also a link called "Intermission," which is a discussion area. The theatre discussion area, for example, didn't have any messages posted from this year when I looked at it. There's not much to look at on these pages. There are a lot of Web discussion boards out there contained within larger sites that get very little activity, simply because most people are not aware they're there. Perhaps, however, you can change that.

FOOTLIGHTS
http://www.footlights.com

A subsidiary of *Playbill,* this magazine has entered the Chicago and Milwaukee markets as a competitor to *Stagebill.* Already there have been some theatres in those markets that offer *Footlights* instead of *Stagebill,* but given the newer nature of *Footlights,* the Web site is still pretty new.

As of this writing, the site was still under construction and the home page said the site should have been complete by March '99, which is why it warrants mention in this book. It appears there will be news and listings offered in two separate sections of the site, one devoted to Chicago and the other devoted to Milwaukee.

NEW YORK THEATRE WIRE
http://www.nytheatre-wire.com/

For those of you who have risked venturing into New York for your acting career, this is a site you have to visit. It's basically advance news of what's playing on New York's stages. Featured on the top of the home page is a link to a page called "Loney's Show Notes" featuring Glenn Loney reviews of New York stage plays. On one particular night I came upon an article on David Hare's play *The Blue Room* starring Nicole Kidman. Loney describes her as wife of "ardent Scientologist and actor Tom Cruise."

As of this writing, the Loney page had twenty-four reviews on it and it was all good reading no matter where you live.

There are also feature articles on the latest plays in New York. The yellow column on the far left features several links, including one for articles by regular columnists, a classified ad section, articles on recordings, articles on New York museums . . . a veritable storehouse of information on what to do in New York, New York.

PERFORMINK
http://www.performink.com

This is the online version of the Chicago-based entertainment trade newspaper covering both film and theatre. It has articles of interest to all actors regardless of whether they live, classified ads with available services for actors, and a detailed listing of all the theatre that's to be seen in Chicago.

THEATRE MANAGEMENT JOURNAL
http://artsnet.heinz.cmu.edu/ATHEEJ/

This site is run by Carnegie-Mellon University and is of interest to those who are involved in arts management. This simple site offers links to articles from the most recent annual print version of the journal, as well as commentary and archived articles from the first issue of the journal.

THEATREWORLD INTERNET MAGAZINE
http://members.aol.com/mouseuk/stage/

This online magazine is a great resource for news, reviews, and listings of theatrical productions in Great Britain, separating news and reviews by regions, the West End and Inner London, then North and South England, among others. If you ever make it to the isle, this is a great site to visit before you go.

THE STAGE
http://www.thestage.co.uk/

This is in the same vein as the Theatreworld site, with news, reviews, and listings of Great Britain's theatre. However, this is an online version of the world's oldest established weekly magazine. There are archives available and even audition listings for actors who choose to perform there.

Overall, online magazines are great resources. Of course, several regular magazines that have entertainment sections also have Web sites, but I don't mention them here because they aren't completely devoted to actor-related subjects. To find them, use the search engines and directories I talk about in Chapter 5.

Theatre Books, Monologues, and Plays 8

W hen it comes to reading, the Web is not going to replace the printed word, in my opinion. You may have heard futurists say that someday the word will only exist in "e-books." This is poppycock. As much that is wonderful about the Web, it still isn't easy to find full-length plays and screenplays or even monologues. In fact, in all my hours of searching for monologues online, I found the only ones that exist are in either unpublished plays or plays that have long since fallen into the public domain, meaning they are so old that their copyright has expired. I haven't found any Tennessee Williams, David Mamet, or Thornton Wilder plays online for your perusal.

Thus, the primary focus of finding plays, screenplays, and books about acting lies in using the Web resources to find those books. Everyone's heard of Amazon.com. I'll tell you about some lesser-known online bookstores that you can visit to find the specific text you're looking for. There are even online bookstores that cater to *you*, the actor. I'll also tell you where to find those plays and screenplays that *are* online.

Let's get started. There are more and more Web sites out there that deal in online commerce, where you can buy books to your heart's delight. We'll start with the one mentioned above.

AMAZON.COM
http://www.amazon.com

In 1998, Amazon.com expanded to offer music and video in order to compete with the multitude of online music and video stores that emerged in the previous year such as Music Boulevard and Reel.com. However, what still distinguishes Amazon.com from its competitors online is its bookstore. Boggling the imagination with more than two million choices, Amazon.com's book-description pages offer both journalistic summaries and reviews, allows the authors to comment on their own work, and lets readers write reviews of books.

It's a very easy site to use, although with the addition of other media for sale, the home page is getting more and more cluttered. However, it does an excellent job of separating its "stores." The major flaw for your purposes is that actual plays published by the likes of Samuel French are not available through this service. More popular plays, such as those by Neil Simon, that have been published by mainstream publishers are available as well as more popular screenplays.

THE INTERNET BOOKSHOP
http://www.bookshop.co.uk

This European site bills itself as the largest online bookshop in Europe, offering more than 1.4 million titles. It's really recommended if you're trying to find, for example, British titles you couldn't otherwise find in the States but you do have to overcome the trouble of converting pounds to dollars. Still, it's easy to use like Amazon.com and is definitely comparable in the number of books offered. Take a look if other methods to find a certain book fail.

ADVANCED BOOK EXCHANGE
http://www.abebooks.com

This is a good site for finding out-of-print books. As you could imagine, books that deal with more specialized material like acting, screenwriting, and films often go out of print after a while, since there often isn't enough demand to warrant second and third printings. Here's where the Advanced Book Exchange comes in. It has a network of participating used-book stores. When you enter the book you're looking for a series of results come up that may match what you're looking for.

Sometimes more than one bookstore has the book you seek

at different prices. The results list where each bookstore is located, what condition the book is in, and the price. If you're not an expert at understanding the value of a used book based on its condition, don't worry about it. If a book costs less than $20 it's usually worth it. After all, it's the content you're really looking for and that never wears out. I have found some old, old used books through this service and saved a lot of time that would have been otherwise been spent crawling through used-book stores in the Chicago area. Then again, you can find some amazing things in used-book stores. I found three film books in Newport, Rhode Island, that I couldn't find anywhere else. You just never know.

The shopping cart format that has become standard on Amazon.com and many other online shopping sites enables the user to choose an item, place it in the shopping cart and then either resume shopping or go to "checkout," at which point the user completes the transaction either with a credit card or a notification that he or she will send a check or money order. At any point while shopping—before you actually check out—you can continue to add or subtract from your shopping cart until you make your final decision on what to buy.

THE INTERNET THEATRE BOOKSHOP
http://ourworld.compuserve.com/homepages/
paul_thain/abooks.htm

This site is associated with Amazon.com. One cool thing about Amazon.com is that it shares its huge database with other Web sites, giving them a commission in exchange for links to the specific book pages on Amazon. It's a way for Webmasters to put online commerce on their site tailored to that Web site's subject. This site is a good place to avoid all the searches you have to do on Amazon.com just to get into your subject area. This site is also associated with the Internet Bookshop in the United Kingdom.

SAMUEL FRENCH
http://www.samuelfrench.com

The grandfather of the theatrical bookshop does have its own Web site and if you need to find a play for monologues or even for your own production you will always come across Samuel French in your search. The company was founded in 1830 by a man named Samuel French and since then it has published innumerable scripts, both produced and unproduced.

There is an online catalog, but it's not as easy to navigate as

Amazon.com or Advanced Book Exchange. Samuel French does not have a "shopping cart" that you can fill and empty at will before submitting your order. Rather, this relatively primitive site provides a catalog with titles and prices and an order form in which you have to type in the names of the books you want. However, as of this writing it did not provide a secure environment for ordering. Most online commerce sites have the option to submit your personal and credit card information on a "secure" site, meaning everything you send will be encrypted. When you enter information that is not secure, anyone else on the Internet could have access to that information. So beware when entering information on this or any other unsecure site. Sometimes it's just easier to call.

BAKER'S PLAYS
http://www.bakersplays.com

This Web site appeals to the same sort who would like Samuel French's Web site, showing off its catalog of books, scripts, and such. The catalog and order form, like Samuel French's, lacks a shopping cart and security, so you submit your credit card information at your own risk.

The best part of the Baker's Plays Web site is the "Theatre Resource Directory," which has a direct URL: *http://www.baker-splays.com/trd/*. It is an online companion to Baker's Plays' print *Theatre Resource Directory,* which, it claims on its site, is sent annually to every educational institution, religious organization, and community theatre in the United States. The online version has a series of links on its home page for resources from box office supplies to wigs. Keep in mind that these lists of resources are far from comprehensive. They often contain names, addresses, Web page URLs and e-mail addresses, and it appears that this information is provided more as an advertisement for the vendors than a resource for you.

BROADWAY PLAY PUBLISHING, INC.
http://www.broadwayplaypubl.com

Broadway Play Publishing, Inc. is a family-owned business and has been around since 1982. It is the third largest play publishing and licensing company based in New York and may very well have the best Web site in its genre. Each play it offers for purchase has its own individual page on the site with a full description and information on the first production of the play if it has been produced yet. The order form is lacking, however, since you basically have to copy the text in the order form and paste it into

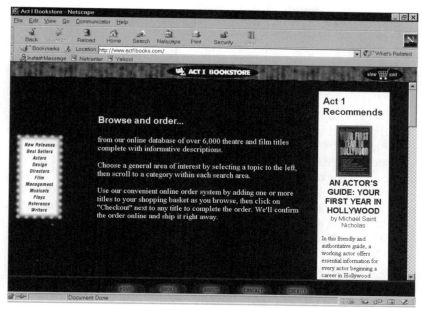

Figure 8–1

an e-mail message. But if you get past that minor annoyance this is a very good source for plays, as well as pages devoted to detailed information on both amateur and professional production rights, competition usage, and restriction lists.

QUITE SPECIFIC MEDIA
http://www.quitespecificmedia.com

Quite Specific Media is a new "umbrella" publishing company consisting of five imprints, including Drama Publishers. There is catalog information but no order form and the site gives an e-mail address only as contact information, so it's hard to tell whether you can even order online. The site does provide phone number. This is a visually appealing site, but there's not much there besides a rough listing of titles and summaries. Still, a title here could appeal to you so the site is worth checking out.

ACT I BOOKSTORE
http://www.act1books.com

In my adored hometown of Chicago—please forgive all biases— we have a wonderful theatre bookstore called Act I, which promotes itself as the largest theatre bookstore in the Midwest.

Offering more than six thousand theatre and film books for purchase, the online shopping guide for the bookstore is very well-designed, utilizing frames to showcase individual books, complete with summaries while allowing you to browse for specific titles and/or subjects at the same time (see Figure 8–1).

You can search by subject for the books that interest you. The subjects are broken down as follows: new releases, best sellers, actors (books for actors), directors (books for directors), film, management, musicals, plays, reference, and writers. After choosing a subject you are given the option of narrowing down your search further. For example, if you choose actors, you can then choose from acting technique, acting business, comedy improv, dialects, and so on. You can also search the subject areas by entering in either keywords or the exact title of the book you're looking for.

The site's shopping cart appears in a separate window each time you add an entry and like most online commerce of this type you can add or subtract any number of items from your shopping cart before you go to the checkout. The checkout area is in another browser window. In the beginning of 1999, the site became secure, making is a safe place to shop.

STAGE & SCREEN BOOK CLUB
http://www.stagenscreen.com

This book club devoted especially to books about the entertainment industry, from film to theatre. It features the old standby for clubs of a similar nature—the "introductory deal." With a membership you can get four books for $1 plus another book free. However, it is extremely unclear what becoming a member entailsand what other financial obligations exist. After much research I learned you are required to buy four more books over the following two years.

According to the FAQ—frequently asked questions page—the Stage & Screen editors review more than one thousand books a year and choose only the best to offer their members, which means if they don't like this book, for example, you won't be able to buy it from them.

The site has a full range of online commerce options, including a shopping cart from which you can remove items if you decide they don't want them. The site is visually attractive. It seems to lean toward promoting published screenplays, which can, of course, have worthy monologues in them. There's also a 10-day "change your mind" refund policy.

AN ANNOTATED BIBLIOGRAPHY OF COMMEDIA DELL'ARTE,
MUSIC HALL, PANTOMIME, AND OTHER DIVERSIONS
http://www.214b.com

This site is a very entertaining look at the performance arts listed above. It also has links to Amazon.com pages that offer books about those disciplines.

THE ASSOCIATION OF AMERICAN UNIVERSITY
PRESSES ONLINE CATALOG
http://aaup.princeton.edu/

This site provides you the opportunity to buy textbooks without taking the classes that usually accompany them. As much as I hate to admit it, there are some very useful and informational textbooks out there.

Not all books published by university presses are "textbooks" per se, but university presses are often more willing to publish books that pertain to very specific interest areas. Therefore, this site offers a fairly broad scope from which to start your search for acting-oriented books and it can sometimes uncover treasures that you wouldn't necessarily find on a site like Amazon.com.

TEXTBOOK CLUB FROM VARSITY BOOKS
http://www.varsitybooks.com/textbookclub/index.asp

This is an attractive site that says it can offer fifteen to forty percent off the price of books sold at college bookstores. There is a shopping cart and a secure online order form. It helps if you know which specific book you're looking for because this online store has an extremely broad scope.

THE ON-LINE BOOKS PAGE
http://www.cs.cmu.edu/books.html

The On-Line Books Page is a guide to books that are available on the Web. The site is without graphics save for the logo but is well laid out site. The home page features links that allow you to search for texts under different parameters: authors, titles, and subjects. There's a guide to new listings and you can also look through the entire database of more than eight thousand titles online. While that sounds like an impressive number, it's dwarfed by the number of real books out there that are lucky enough to be protected by copyright. Hence, the books you read here are in the public domain, which means they're either more than seventy-five years old or their copyrights were never renewed.

When you choose a title, you have the option of downloading the text as a text file or as a Zip file. A text file will load into your browser as if it's a Web page. You can either read the text on your browser or use my method, which is to copy and paste the manuscript into whichever word processing or text reader program—for example, Windows' Notepad—you use, change the font to whatever best suits you for readability, and save it.

It's probably not a good idea to print out entire books with your printer. When I linked to *The Secret Places of The Heart* by H.G. Wells and pasted it into Word, I came up with eighty-six single-spaced pages of slightly more than sixty-seven thousand words. Another problem is that formatting does not always survive pasting into a word processor, meaning paragraph indentations could disappear. If you hate this, it's best to save the text in your text reader, or just save the text and open it in your Web browser.

Just a glance through the new listings shows the site updates this page often. There's also a news section. When I looked at the site, there was a story on the twenty-year copyright extension that has gone into law. There are feature stories on subjects like women writers and banned books online. And there are updates on online books that have been requested and those projects that are in progress.

I'm not sure how useful this site is for the average actor. However, you should always look for new sources of ideas and even monologues. Wells' *Secret Places of the Heart* may not contain suitable monologue material but your theatre company could find it adaptable to the stage.

THE COMPLETE WORKS OF WILLIAM SHAKESPEARE
http://www-tech.mit.edu/Shakespeare/works.html

This site provides every work by William Shakespeare online for your perusal. The titles of his tragedies, comedies, histories, and sonnets are listed in an easy-to-read fashion, separated into those categories based on the electronic Moby edition of the complete works.

For example, I clicked on the title of *Hamlet*. The front page of the Hamlet portion of the site is a simple list of the acts and scenes. Each scene name is a link to the page that contains of the entire contents of that scene. You have the option of loading the entire play onto one very, very long Web page.

There's also a guide to Bartlett's list of Shakespearean quotations if that's all you're looking for.

There's also a page containing links to other Shakespeare resources on the Web, as well as a Shakespeare discussion board. When I looked at the site early this year, it appeared to have last been updated at the end of 1996, so don't expect any revolutionary things to happen on this site. It's simply a good place to obtain all of Shakespeare's works.

BIBLIOBYTES
http://www.bb.com

This site offers online books under a multitude of subjects, ready for you to read right on the Web. Subject areas range from "Adventure" to "Young Adult." I chose search the "Plays" category. Forty-eight links to complete plays online came up. Most of them were Shakespeare, probably because the copyrights have expired. Old translations of men longer dead, such as Aeschylus and Aristophanes are also included. You won't find any modern playwrights represented on this page.

The value of BiblioBytes, or any long online text, depends on your tolerance for reading text on your glowing computer screen for long periods of time. Also, only about three hundred words appear per Web page before you have to hit "next page." Unfortunately, this means you have to remain online if you want to read any large portion of a book or play. Thus, it is really only recommended if you have a cable modem connection or dedicated connection at your day job, or if you don't mind tying up your phone line for a long time.

ON-LINE SCRIPT SHOWCASE
http://www.newplays.com

This Web site begins rather unusually, with a series of pages displaying abstract drawings beckoning you to continue turning pages until you finally reach a page with real content. Once you finally get through the pretentious murk about what great art you're about to see, you reach a series of links to excerpts from samples.

THE DRAMATIC EXCHANGE: CATALOG OF PLAYS
http://www.dramex.org/htmlplays.html

This is a site that has full plays available online. The selection is much greater than the On-Line Script Showcase and you can get to the links and the plays much more quickly. The plays themselves are available in text format or Microsoft Works format. You're not going to find Tennessee Williams or Thornton Wilder here. Rather, you'll find unproduced or ancient plays the likes of Homer. The plays also each have a SIF—summary information file—that gives a quick summary of the play with character description, running time, and information on how to contact the playwright. The site has a simple layout, and you may just find a gem here if you look hard enough.

THE ONLINE SCRIPTHOUSE
http://www.scripthouse.cjb.net

This site is very well crafted, another source for online scripts. This site is brand new and as of July, 1999, they only have six online scripts in their arsenal. However, you should check this site out for any additional scripts become available to look at or if you or your pals are interested in submitting scripts for world-wide perusal.

SCRIPT WORLD
http://www.screenwriter.com/scriptworld.html

If you have seen a film recently that has the monologue of your dreams, you might try Script World. This online commerce center sells screenplays from *All About Eve* to *Zorro: The Gay Blade*. It charges $15 per screenplay, which is reasonable as long as you know what you want out of the screenplay. You can either pay by credit card online or pay by check, mailing it with the printed online form. Since there doesn't appear to be a secure order form, I'd suggest you just mail the form with a check.

Unions And Organizations 9

*J*ack Nicholson had to wear a prosthetic nose when he played Jimmy Hoffa in the 1992 film *Hoffa*. Now that's an actor! He did, however, have something in common with Hoffa in that both were members of unions.

The great part of the Web, especially in this context, is that you have immediate access to information that would ordinarily take some time to retrieve. You don't have to call your local Actor's Equity office or ask for the counsel of your fellow actors to get information on how to join that union. Now all you have to do is log onto the Equity site and everything you need to get started is right there.

Still, it wasn't until after I was beginning this book that Actors' Equity even had its own Web site. There was some information here and there from local offices but nothing from the parent organization. But in December 1998, the site finally appeared and is already one of the finest actors resource on the Web.

ACTORS' EQUITY ASSOCIATION
http://www.actorsequity.org

Actors Equity, as its Web site explains, was

founded in 1913, is the labor union representing actors and stage managers in the legitimate theatre in the

United States. Equity negotiates minimum wages and working conditions, administers contracts, and enforces the pro-
visions of its various agreements with theatrical employers.
There are currently about 40,000 active Equity members.

It took Actors' Equity a long time to establish its own Web site. While
writing columns on entertainment Web sites since 1996, I was
always baffled that AEA didn't have a presence on the Internet. But
come the end of 1998, the day had finally arrived.

In the December 4, 1998, issue of Chicago's *PerformInk*, Kathryn
V. Lamkey, central regional director, introduced the new Web site:

> Don't worry, it doesn't know if your dues are paid or even if
> you're a member. It is meant to serve as an industry source of
> information. It is designed to be of use to Equity members,
> non-Equity actors and stage managers, Equity and non-Equity
> producers, theatre students and even the general public.

Indeed, the new Web site is pretty impressive as a resource for all
comers. The home page has a large graphic of the word "ACTORS."
Each letter leads you to a different part of the site. When you move
your cursor over each letter, it becomes transparent, revealing the
subject of the page to which you are about to link. Pretty cool.

"A" leads you to the page "About Equity." Just this section is
enough to fill an entire site. It begins with the short introduction
quoted above, followed by a greeting by the president of AEA and the
Webmaster of the page. There's an article about how Equity works.
It explains how AEA is governed within the National Council and
Regional Boards and also includes a link to the group's *entire* constitution and bylaws. Then, it details the specifics of how one can join
Actors' Equity, and what you have to pay once you join. There's even
a picture of the treasured Equity card. There's a list of regions and
offices and an interesting page that gives the history of AEA, from its
founding in 1913, to the first strike by theatrical performers in 1919,
to today. There's a frequently asked questions page and a list of
union affiliations.

Going back to the front page of the site, when you click on the
"C" in ACTORS, the "Casting Call" page appears. The page proclaims,
"Each week Equity theatrical producers nationwide post job notices
for actors, dancers, singers, and stage managers." It allows you to
search Equity's national database. There is a brief overview explaining that these auditions are Equity auditions, so if your little cousin
Mac with the funny hair wants to audition for something, this isn't
the place to look. But if *you* are Equity, audition notices are available
on a nationwide scale or a state-by-state scale. When I selected

"Illinois," quite a few results came back. You can link to a page with as many details you need regarding any single audition, including producer/theatre, contract type, date, time, and place for interview. It's an outstanding feature of the site and *the* place to look for audition notices if you're Equity.

Back to the "T" in ACTORS: The "Theatre News" page is, again, a fine site on its own. The home page is a simple list of headlines that link you to articles. There's also "Show Buzz," a column that offers little one-sentence snippets on notable theatrical productions. There's an advice column titled "Ask George Spelvin." There are "Regional Reports" with profiles on specific cities. When I checked it out, there was an article on "Cleveland, Renaissance City." There's a heck of a lot to read in the "Theatre News" section.

The "O" in ACTORS leads you to "Onstage/Offstage." The only content in this section when I accessed it was a profile of Robert Prosky talking about what it is to be an actor. Presumably there will be more profiles as this page continues to grow.

The "R" in ACTORS leads you to the "Resource Center." It contains lists of AEA offices, area liaisons, and related Web sites; another link to the constitution and bylaws; and another link to the FAQ page. When I accessed the page, AEA promised it would soon offer "downloadable forms, a glossary of Equity terms, press releases, and more." That might just be there by the time you read this.

Finally, the "S" takes you to the page that displays "Services for You." It is a list of services and benefits provided by or negotiated by Equity. There's a detailed summary of equity agreements and codes for contracts, description of pensions and health funds, unemployment and workmen's compensation, and income tax assistance. There is a list of equity-affiliated organizations as well.

Overall, the site is fabulous and just about worth the long wait. As of this writing, the site was only a couple of months old, so there will probably be plenty more to look at than what I've described here, but this is already the only place on the Web you can go to learn everything you need to know about becoming Equity and maintaining your career once you go Equity. It's a must on your bookmark list.

SCREEN ACTORS GUILD
http://www.sag.com

After hearing all my compliments of the Actors' Equity site, you're probably prepared for me to trash SAG's site. Not so! While not as richly detailed as the Equity site, the SAG site is far from useless and is really quite comparable to the Equity site. When I looked at the site on January 21, 1999, it had an enormous headline regarding the SAG–AFTRA merger vote. It linked to a series of pages that were relevant to the merger vote, including the letter from the president of SAG explaining in detail why he thought SAG members should vote for the merger. Once the merger was voted down at the end of January, the page was quickly updated with stories on the vote as well as a letter from the SAG president saying everything was going to be fine.

There was a page on "Answering the Anti-Merger Myths" as well. Those pages will most likely disappear by the time you read this. But that shows that the page is updated on a regular basis. Actors need to have quick, easy access to information, especially information this critical to the union.

The home page of the site is a graphic of a movie theatre with links to the various pages within the site displayed on the screen. The first link is to the "Guild Member Area." One part of the member area is ntitled "For Members Only: The Basics." It features a comprehensive SAG directory of all kinds of offices, a glossary of filmmaking terms titled "Terminology of the Craft," a history of SAG called "The SAG Story: From Minimum Wage to the Digital Age," and a series of press materials including *Screen Actor Magazine.*

"Information for Filmmakers" is a link on the main screen that's a great information storehouse for those filmmakers that want to learn about SAG's agreements and rules. "SAG in The Spotlight" is a series of press releases about SAG's community work.

"So You Wanna Be An Actor?" is a link on the main screen that should help you begin your career. It starts with the traditional warnings that on average actors make no money. It then goes through articles detailing the processes you go through in eventually becoming a full-time SAG actor. There's also a page with information on the SAG Awards, a greeting page from SAG President Richard Masur, and a links page.

SAG-PPHP HOME PAGE
http://www.sagph.org/

This is the official Web site for the Screen Actors Guild–Producer Pension and Health Plans. There are online versions of the last three years' worth of *Take 2* newsletters, the official quarterly newsletter of the SAG-PPHP. There is an individual page with information on the health plan, recently updated, detailing eligibility, various benefits, and how to file a claim. The pension plan page has information on minimum earning requirements, types of pension, and forms of pension payment.

Other pages include a directory, a guide to the board of trustees, and a page of general information covering such topics as "How to Appeal a Denial of Benefits" and "The Importance of Filing a Master Data Card." This is hardly a glamorous page, but if you want to be covered by a plan for SAG members, you should see this site. It contains some important information.

AFTRA

http://www.aftra.org

This site explains that AFTRA represents its members in four major areas: news and broadcasting; entertainment programming; the recording business; and commercials and nonbroadcast, industrial, educational media (see Figure 9–1).

Like the SAG site, the AFTRA site is a fabulous place to find out everything you ever wanted to know about a union but were afraid to ask. Just the "What is AFTRA?" section gives you information on all the health plans and coverage, AFTRA contracts, and governance and administration.

The site is also split up into the four major areas. The news and broadcasting area, for example, has its own self-contained page with specific information on contracts, negotiation updates, a list of the

Figure 4–2

broadcast steering committee, and a job board. This is a great way to get the information you want in your area without having to browse through irrelevant details.

Also, in the main site, there is a complete list of AFTRA-franchised agents. You can narrow your search by clicking on a specific city name.

The site's resources page has links to an AFTRA national directory, a list of the Eastern and Western Section National Boards, the national schedule, local offices, and publications. You can read press releases announcing the latest votes by AFTRA members. There's information on the AFTRA/Heller Memorial Foundation Scholarships as well as an application to print out and mail. A legislative update page alerts AFTRA members of legislation that affects them. An example of one such update is an article on a bankruptcy law in Congress that would deny artists specific rights in declaring bankruptcy that are reserved for people in the "real world."

Like most sites, there's a FAQ page and links page.

CANADIAN ACTORS' EQUITY ASSOCIATION
http://www.caea.com/

This site has been up much longer than the site of the CAEA's compatriots to the south and features the same kind of wealth of information that is incredibly valuable, especially if you end up in Toronto, which is a thriving theatre town despite Livent's teetering collapse.

There are detailed pages on who CAEA is, how to join, benefits of membership, how it's governed, etc. There's an "Auditions" page explaining CAEA auditions. There are job listings for nonacting theatre jobs, a CAEA management list, a list of CAEA agreements and, of course, a links page as well as numerous other features. It's a very informative site.

AFL-CIO
http://www.aflcio.org

With a much more political bent, this Web site is worth looking at, especially if you really want to get more involved with SAG, AFTRA or Equity. The American Federation of Labor and Congress of Industrial Organizations is the grandfather, grandmother, and big brother to just about every union in the nation, including SAG, AFTRA, and Equity. I won't go into detail about the site except to say it is an excellent site containing all the information you need to become the next Norma Rae.

Casting Online

A fter you've made the irrevocable decision to become an actor, you then have to learn how to beg for food. Or at least beg for work. Going through the process of getting an agent, auditioning, and generally feeling lower than a worm is all normal in the quest for superstardom. It would help you out enormously if the Internet would make things much easier for you to forge ahead in your career.

Unfortunately, it doesn't yet. And how much it eventually will is completely unknown. The age-old process of auditioning, sending out your headshots, and withering in shame has been a part of the actor's life for eons and will remain so. In this context, you want to think of the Internet as a time-saving resource. When you end up spending money to have your headshot posted on a Web page, you have to ask yourself what you're getting for your money. Things like headshots are necessary expenditures.

You're also aware that the casting process has involved actual human contact for hundreds of years. But, since the Web has grown, several Web sites have tried to convince actors that, for a small fee, their headshots and resumes can be posted to a Web page for millions to see and enjoy, and ultimately capture them roles. Unfortunately, these public Web sites have never done much. When I looked at some of these sites, I often found there were no actors on them! And I wonder what kind of motivation there is for a casting director or agent to do a talent search on a Web site when there are only three actors on the site. Well, if anyone is really looking, it's someone with time on his or her hands.

But that's not to say companies haven't tried to offer an Internet casting solution. One could say two generations of casting Web sites coexist for now. There are public Web sites that anyone can visit to check out headshots and resumes like those mention above. Then there are newer sites that have taken advantage of the newer Web browsers that support usernames and passwords. These are secure sites that are only accessible to casting directors and talent agents. They sign up for the service, receive their usernames and passwords, and head off on their talent hunt.

It sounds like an excellent idea, but at the beginning of 1999, how many people were using it? In a November 1998 article on the subject in *Hollywood Reporter*, Karen Stuart, executive director of the Association of Talent Agents explained, "We're in a little catch-22 right now. A lot of casting directors and agents are upgrading their equipment and learning the Internet, but the casting directors are saying there aren't enough agents on the other end, and my members are saying there aren't enough casting directors looking at it."

According to an exclusive *Backstage West/DramaLogue* poll, both sides are using online services but not with a great deal of enthusiasm just yet. Eighty-four percent of the casting directors asked said they used the Internet and on average, they estimated they did about 19.4 percent of their business online. Only 78 percent of agents polled said they used the Internet at all and those that used the Internet said they averaged about 20.7 percent of their work online.

With the few sites that provide secure access for casting directors and agents, it's really the actor that drives this process. On a site like CastNet, the service may have access to the material provided by an agent who has affiliated him- or herself with the service, but the actor's headshots, resume, and potential demo reel can't be posted until the actors join the services. And that costs money. Not an overwhelming amount, mind you, but it can often run you at least $100 a year depending on the service—

enough to motivate you to keep both eyes open when you surf these sites.

Still, thorough research is important. In Chicago, for example, talent representative Diane Herro Sanford would not sign up with the CastNet Web site because she didn't "want to be in the position of forcing [actors] to do this. If they want to sign up, it should be their choice."

The general consensus is that you will still have to go to a photo service to get your headshots printed, you will still have to have copies of your resume made, and you will still have to buy staples with which you can affix your resume to the back of your printed headshot. These are not bad things. You cannot afford to blindly sign up for each of these services without also doing things the old-fashioned way with faxes and mailings. If you are not in one of the major markets, especially L.A., it's foolhardy to attempt to spend any money on these Web sites. A service like The Link only services Los Angeles and New York. CastNet services Los Angeles only and has recently broken into the Chicago market. These are not answers.

If there's one hope for these Internet services, it can best be summed up in the words of Bob Mohler, director of sales and marketing at CastNet, who said the company's goal when one of its clients moved offices, was for them to come and say, "I need my phone. I need my fax machine and I need CastNet."

"First Generation" Sites

So where did all these sites come from and what are they hoping to accomplish? First, I'm going to tell you about what I call the "first generation" casting sites, where headshots and resumes are made available for viewing without the need for a username or password. See Appendix 1 for URLs to the sites in this chapter.

BuzzNYC/BuzzLA

This Web site functions both as a resource center for actors and a place where agents and casting directors can look for talent. The home page of Buzz contains two links that give you the option of looking for talent or adding your name to the roster.

This site has been around since before the advent of the secure casting pages so anyone, regardless of affiliation, can access the talent search pages.

When I clicked on the link "I'm looking for talent," it opened a newspaper-style front page that gave me the option of searching for the name of a specific actor or making a general search through the database.

The search page has pull-down menus that give you multiple-choice options, so you don't get to enter your own specific criteria. For location, you can either choose New York or Los Angeles. Under union status, you can choose AEA, non-AEA, SAG, or non-SAG. For sex, you can choose both, male, or female. There are six age ranges and five choices for ethnicity.

There are also two different ways you can view the data: list system and Java Script browser. The list system is not very helpful. It's a quick recap of names, heights, weights, genders, and union affiliations. Thus, you don't get to see the thumbnail-size headshots. The Java Script browser only works with Netscape. So, if you're in Netscape and choose the Java Script browser, you will see a framed Web page for an individual actor. There are buttons in the left frame that give you the chance to see the headshot, which pops up in a separate little window, and give you the option of moving on to the next actor or further defining your search parameters.

I chose SAG talent in New York City, both genders, all ethnicities, between the ages of eighteen and twenty-five. I got back fourteen caucasian women, five caucasian men, three African American women, no African American men, two Hispanic women, no Hispanic men, no Asians of either gender and one "Other" in each gender. It's not exactly a definitive list of young actors in New York City. Still, this provides you, the actor, with a chance to stick out from the crowd.

On the other side of the site, actors can click on "I'm an actor" on the home page and can list off Off Broadway shows in New York for free—and it does stress, New York only, so you Nebraskan actors can't list your latest production of *Our Town*. In a bit of false advertising, the actor's front page claims it offers a link to entertainment news, but it just connects to a page with links to unaffiliated entertainment news sites.

The frustrating part of the site is that it has no information on how you as an actor can post your headshot and resume on the talent page.

The Film, TV and Commercial Employment Network

This Web site caters to talent both in front of and behind the camera. The home page isn't the most attractive one I've seen, but you should know not to judge a Web site by its home page.

The site is split up into different sections that you may be interested in depending on your area of expertise. The section I'm going to concentrate on is called "Actors Now." The link from the home page is rather vague, telling you to click on the link if you're an agent or casting director. It isn't immediately clear where on the home page actors should click.

When you reach the "Actors Now" page, you can click on either "Men" or "Women." When I looked at this site, there were a total of five men and six women listed. Hardly worth a casting director's time! There are no search parameters set up here, nor are there usernames or passwords to keep the site secure.

If you're interested in having your headshot and resume posted on the site, there's a link to an informational page. There are a couple of testimonials of the few actors that appear on the site saying their presence on the site landed them auditions. The charge for the service is a little less than other services, at $65 a year.

There's also an order form for ordering literature that's discussed in other areas of the site, but the order form is not secure. Therefore, it is probably better to just call the phone number listed on the site if you're interested in these materials.

Talentworks

Talentworks is a very professional-looking site that has a few hitches in its programming. If you click the link to the "About Talentworks" page from the home page and then click "Home" to return to the home page, you get a message saying the page cannot be found. No matter how good a site is, it can be spoiled by basic programming mistakes like this that would be solved in five seconds.

Talentworks offers membership to individual actors and also to talent agencies. It costs $50 a year to post your headshot and resume on this site. This service gives you the ability to directly update your resume from your Web browser, effectively giving you your own home page on its site, which is a nice feature.

It also has a useful search feature that allows casting directors to enter search criteria and come up with results based on certain keywords. Talentworks uses each word of your resume when performing a search.

It also offers a ten-day free trial, but unfortunately, since the site is not secure, the registration form for the free trial still requires your credit card information.

SHOWBIZJOBS.COM

This Web site describes itself as "a membership of recruitment managers from leading Companies in the film, television, recording and attractions industries who seek quality candidates for a multitude of industry-related positions." This means, of course, that this Web site is not even remotely exclusive to actors, but my philosophy is that I don't rule out any job that has the potential of feeding and clothing you.

Job searches are limited to the Los Angeles and New York areas. The search page has pull-down menus that allow you to narrow your search by a category, ranging from Accounting to Web Development. You can also narrow your search by specific companies as well as posting dates. Underneath all these menu selections are logos of entertainment companies that have a certain number of job listings that you can look up. So, if your dream is to have a job with MGM, you can look here.

NATIONAL TALENT POOL

One of the more interesting sites out of the "first generation" sites listed here is based out of Chicago. It's brought to Chicagoans by one of the leading photo services in Chicago: National Photo Service. The Talent Pool is a free service for those actors who reproduce their headshots at their National Photo Service's shop (minimum of one hundred). Those who wish to participate in the Talent Pool but do not use at National Photo can join for six months for $40 or for an annual fee of $65.

The site's home page offers quite a few links. The "Actor's Call Board" is a message board with postings relevant to working actors in Chicago. The majority of postings I saw as of this writing were put up by little independent filmmakers seeking actors for their short films. "Audition Tips" is a clear, concise, and helpful collection of tips from panelists at National Photo's annual audition clinic. "Auditions" is a simple posting of Chicago-area auditions.

Second Generation Sites

The "second generation" of casting Web sites offers secure access for agents and casting directors. These are intended for the serious actor in L.A., New York—and in the case of CastNet, Chicago—who won't just fork over cash to some Web site just because it's supposed to be the wave of the future.

TALENTSCENE

This particular site is run by a company called LINETV and its intention is to provide the resource of a casting center on the Internet. You need to register with a username and password and preferably be a casting director or agent in order to view actors.

When searching for actors on this site I again wanted to use the widest possible parameters: women aged eleven to eighty. But when I tried to search by age, it was not an option so I just searched for women with no other criteria. I came up with a total of twenty-five names. This may not provide enough of a selection, making it less of a comprehensive resource.

When I last looked, there was a limited-time offer that let actors post their headshot and resume at no charge.

CAST-A-HEAD

This is a New York-based Web site, protected by username and password for casting directors. So, if you live in New York or are about to go to New York, make sure you look at this site. It is similar in function to the Talent Scene site. Like many of this nature, the site is split into two sections: one for casting directors and agents and one for talent. I'll tell you about the talent section, which you're interested in because you're talent.

First, there's a complete list of agents in New York who are affiliated with SAG, AFTRA or AEA. Very useful. Then there's a link to books about acting and the entertainment industry that you can purchase.

Following those is a link to audition notices. The notices are all separated into logical categories, from which you link to the notices themselves. The categories are split into "stage" and "TV/film." Under "stage" there are listings for non-AEA auditions, AEA auditions, chorus auditions and others. Under "TV/film" there are listings for SAG, non-SAG . . . you get the idea.

Then you link to information on how casting directors and agents view headshots and resumes on this site. Those who are looking for talent will first see "thumbnail" versions of your headshots because they are small and load quickly. Clicking on a thumbnail connects the viewer to a bigger headshot and a resume. Also, if the actor is currently appearing on stage, television, or film, a nice little "Now Appearing" logo appears above the headshot linking to information on what project he or she is currently involved in.

The feature called "QuickRes" enables someone looking for talent to send search parameters to Cast-A-Head, for example, a male who is between five feet eleven inches and six feet one inch tall. Whenever the search engine comes upon these criteria, it will notify that person. When conducting a search, the program looks at every word in every resume.

Membership in Cast-A-Head is $100 per year and includes up to three headshots, a resume, unlimited updates, and activation of the "NowAppearing" marquee upon request. Additional headshots are $10 each and an audio reel of up to one minute can be included for $49.95. To register you must fill out the form, print it out, and send it by mail along with your headshot(s) and resume.

CASTNET

Probably the most ambitious of all of these Web sites is CastNet (see Figure 10–1). As Richard Horgan of CastNet explained in my interview with him, the concept of CastNet began in 1988 as an idea Frank Zappa, of all people, had while he was sitting on a couch with Jay Sloatman. Zappa mentioned that it would be cool if casting directors, agents, and actors could be linked electronically. So, according to Horgan, "From that conversation on the couch with Frank Zappa, his mind started. 'All right, let me figure this out.' He started with video digitizing boards, then on to the CD-ROMs, kind of like a mad scientist in the laboratory he tried all this stuff."

Eventually, the World Wide Web appeared and the vision of CastNet began to take form. After years of preparation, the site became fully active for Los Angeles casting directors, agents, and talent in August 1997. In 1998, CastNet entered the rich theatre and commercial marketplace of Chicago. CastNet's goal is to have fifty-seven thousand actors registered in its database by the end of 1999.

Welcome to Castnet.com®, a state-of-the-art secured online casting and submission service. Castnet.com® is a highly secured, restricted-access system. The service is available to: casting directors who are members of the **C.S.A. (Casting Society of America), the C.C.D.A. (Commercial Casting Directors Association)** or are verified independents; and to talent agencies that are currently franchised by the **Screen Actors Guild.**

Castnet.com® uses its own virtual private network to offer non-Internet dependent connectivity to its high-end entertainment industry users. The system was developed over several years prior to its initial launch on October 1, 1996.

Castnet.com® is in the process of merging with The Entertainment Internet, a publicly traded company. To obtain a current quote of symbol: EINI, please click here. To view some of the recent media coverage about Castnet.com®, please go to our Press Room.

Castnet.com ® is best viewed with Netscape Navigator (v. 3.0 or above) or Internet Explorer (v. 4.0 or above).

Castnet.com®, 5820 Wilshire Boulevard, Suite #605, Los Angeles, CA 90036
Tel: 323-964-4900 | Fax: 323-964-1050 | Email: castnet@castnet.com
© 1999, The Entertainment Internet, Inc., a publicly traded company.
All rights reserved.

Figure 10–1

It gears access only toward CSA/CCDA casting directors, who can make their way through the site and find you.

So how do you get into CastNet? The site is very secure, with usernames and passwords for agents and casting directors alike. The home page makes the split between the two portions of site immediate. The area for casting directors and agents is pretty much inaccessible to anyone else. In a little bit, I'll go over what those folks see when they visit their part of the site.

The actors portion of CastNet opens immediately into the "About Us" section of the site, explaining that CastNet is used by more than 32,000 professional actors, 200 casting directors, and

120 guild-franchised talent agencies. These numbers will likely have increased by the time you read this.

There's a link from that page that connects to an overview of the benefits of joining. Some of the more interesting aspects to a membership are free mailing labels for L.A., New York, and Chicago casting directors. Sides are available from the actors portion of the Web site or you could have them faxed directly to you. The site provides a place where you can create a postcard to remind casting directors of your latest project, and CastNet will send it to all the casting directors using the service. The company also offers free seminars and workshops for actors Wednesdays and Saturdays at its offices, but they are in Los Angeles because all of the offices are there.

There's also a page called "Actors Forum," which is basically a message board much like the ones you see in newsgroups and other Web pages.

Now on the other, secure part of the site, casting directors can enter criteria for a talent search and the site will display a series of thumbnail-sized headshots. Agents, who have their own distinct access, can look at those criteria as well and submit their actors.

But there's one drawback. Even if your agent is signed up with CastNet, you need to sign up yourself to be able to appear on the site. And you have to pay, as I'm sure you've guessed by now, which means you have to pay for your agents to represent you online.

In the following excerpt from a December 4, 1998, column I cowrote with Carrie L. Kaufman in Chicago's *PerformInk* newspaper we explain that

> Bob Mohler, director of sales and marketing for CastNet, says that CastNet takes the legal right to work very seriously and does not encourage agents or casting directors to stop taking paper headshots and resumes. Nor do they encourage agents and casting directors to stop talking to each other. Mohler points out, though, that agents often "suggest" their clients pay money to be listed in a headshot directory or subscribe to various trade publications. Rightly or wrongly, actors often act on these suggestions out of fear that if they don't, the agent will not think that they are serious and will not send them out.

Actors must pay a $99.95 annual fee for posting a resume and headshot posted or a $189.95 yearly fee for three headshots along with a one-minute video clip, and audio and video demo reels. The company just introduced a new $12.95 per month plan, and Mohler has said that prices may change, so it behooves you to check out the CastNet site periodically just to keep abreast of changes.

EXTRACAST

This web site specializes in casting extras online. It promotes itself as "California's Exclusive On-Line Background Performers Resource." ExtraCast was founded in 1996 and was incorporated in September 1997. It exists as a resource mainly for background casting directors, and it claims it casts a higher percentage of actors than any other online casting service. Membership costs $55 and only certified casting directors have access to the casting page. The company operates out of the strange land called Beverly Hills and membership is only available to residents of California.

The home page is catchy and attractive, with a left-hand column full of testimonials from casting directors praising the site's merits. In the middle of the page is a list of the site's sections.

There's a "visitors" section that allows you to see an example of an "Extra Zed," as Extracast calls it. It can feature an animated rotation of up to three photos of yourself, as well as the normal information, special skills, and even automobiles owned, if you'd like your car to be an extra!

Another feature you can access from the home page is "ExtraChat." This is a members-only area that allows you to chat with other members. It also offers "ExtraBeep" on the site, where casting directors can page you directly from your Extracast Web page. That particular part of the service costs $20 for six months and you can use your existing pager.

And, of course, there's a page of "ExtraLinks," which is a short but great list of industry-related links, all of which are covered in this volume.

ACADEMY OF MOTION PICTURES ARTS AND SCIENCES PLAYERS
DIRECTORY AND THE LINK

Along with CastNet, the Link provides the strongest argument for actors to spend money peddling their wares on the Internet. The Link is the result of an alliance between the Academy of Motion

Picture Arts and Sciences Players Directory and Breakdown Services Limited.

When Hollywood reached its enormous boom period of the 1930s, the Academy decided to publish a casting directory. The first issue of the *Players Directory of the Academy* appeared in 1937. The site explains "That first issue of the Players Directory included photos and information on about 1,200 actors. 60 years later, more than 16,000 of their contemporary brethren find their way into the Directory on a regular basis."

If you are SAG, AFTRA, or AEA, you can appear in the next issue of the *Players Directory* for $25, and, more importantly in the context of our subject, also be eligible to be submitted by your agent to The Link for roles in the breakdowns.

As The Link's Information page explains,

> In July 1996, the Academy and Breakdown Services, Ltd., which supplies the entertainment industry with daily information about available acting roles, forged an alliance to develop new ways for agents and casting directors to do their jobs, utilizing rapidly changing technological tools.
>
> The resulting new electronic system, The Link, which was introduced in March of 1997, streamlines the photo submission process between talent agents and casting directors. Under the new system, Breakdown Services electronically transmits its daily breakdowns of available acting roles to its agent clients. Using the photos and resumes from the Players Directory, those agents may then electronically transmit to casting directors the names of talent that they would like to see considered for the roles described in the breakdowns. As the incoming e-mail-like transmission links with the casting director's computer, he or she will find the submitted actor's photo and resume. In the past, this process has happened through the physical delivery of paper and photos, using messengers and taking several hours.
>
> The Academy/Breakdown alliance The Link is an important step for the Academy as it continues to implement its plans to make the Players Directory an even more effective resource for the acting and production communities. Further technological advances will allow video and audio clips.
>
> These advances will not only save time and money, but will increase opportunities for the actors listed in the Directory. As technology changes, so will the Directory, with

one goal in mind: to provide the best possible resource for the industry.

The Link, like CastNet and Cast-a-Head, is a secure Web site, but it does offer a link—all puns thereof are not intended—to a "practice session." The practice session allows you to exist as a talent representative of film stars in the late 1930s, a Max Pennington of International Artists Agency. Or you could exist as casting director David Selznick, attempting to cast a little film called *Gone With the Wind*. This shows you what a casting director or agent looks at when they visit the site, giving you a clearer idea of its usefulness.

You can go to the Players Directory itself for information on how to be included. That site looks very similar to The Link page, telling visitors all about the Players Directory and how to submit their resumes as well.

If you're in L.A. and want to pursue a career in film acting, it is imperative that you check these out.

CASTING AND MEDIA ON-LINE, INC. (CAMEO)

CAMEO is another member of the growing list of Web sites that offer secure access for casting directors and agencies to search for talent. On the "About CAMEO" page the company states that

> The CAMEO system is significantly different from other online "talent banks." It is unique in that it is far more than an online database—it is *a complete system* designed specifically to automate the flow of information between casting directors, talent agencies, production companies, advertising agencies, and much more. It incorporates a multi-window multi-tasking interface that is familiar and friendly to users.

The company believes that the World Wide Web "page flipping" format is not a viable form of direct communication between users of a single database, arguing that with so many browsers, Java applets, plug-ins, and the like, it is not a suitable platform from which to provide a suitable interface.

Thus, the company has come up with its own software for you to use, which is called FirstClass groupware. It only offers the service to union-affiliated actors, so if you're not in a union you should join one.

The number of casting sites will only grow, most likely, and those that do enter the Internet market will most likely follow the lead of professional industry services like The Link and CastNet. Consult people you know—your agent and fellow actors—about which sites to tour. I would recommend trying out one of the sites available above if you live in L.A., New York, or Chicago— remembering that some sites service some cities and not others— making sure you don't invest in too much too soon.

Dance 11

I know what you're thinking. You're looking at this chapter title and wonder why dance is included in *The Actor's Guide to the Internet*. Well, dancers can act. And actors can dance. While the art of the American musical theatre is hardly at the heights it once was half a century ago, there is a kind of renaissance right now with shows like *Rent* and *Ragtime* among others. Plus, there are plenty of actors who practice more than one discipline, and it's always good to have as many tricks in your bag as possible.

So I'm going to skim through some of the more basic resource Web sites for dancers, places you can start on your search for sites for actors. In my search for pages, I found mostly sites for dance companies and recreational dance sites. But you aren't going to find country line-dancing classes listed here. Even if you aren't a dancer, there are still some very interesting sites to check out.

SAPPHIRE SWAN DANCE DIRECTORY
http://www.sapphireswan.com/dance/

This site is a comprehensive links site, made up of frames. The left frame lists links to sites covering numerous styles of dance, from Balkan to Flamenco to Samba to Scottish.

Once you link on the style, a list of links pertaining to that style appears in the main frame.

Meanwhile, on the upper frame you have the choice of following links to dance pages that are not specific to style. These are grouped under the heading "Other Dance Links." the links connect you to sites that cover dance books, dance schools, dance supplies, other dance links and other dance directories.

The site is far from flashy—there are very few graphics involved—but the key is it will connect you to dance sites a lot faster than Yahoo! or Excite.

DANCE ONLINE
http://www.danceonline.com

This site is polished, professional, and very attractive, with its home page featuring some very subtle little "MouseOver" animations, which animate when you place your cursor over them. The subtitle of the site is "New Dance From Around the World." And its intention is to create a definitive online presence for contemporary dance (see Figure 11–1).

There's a list of links to pages that begins with the "Features" page. An incredibly cool feature to see, if you have a fast enough modem, is a RealVideo presentation that the site will keep as a regular feature. This is streaming video, meaning you can see it as it comes through your computer. It's called "Dance on the Web." The first installment was up on the site when I saw it, called, "*(voice tells)* fourteen tiny pictures, no more, no less." from Jennifer Lacey and Zeena Parkins. The page says "*(voice tells)* . . . is composed of rich, distilled fragments that acquire and change identity through accumulation" and features a review snippet from the Village Voice on Lacey's work.

This particular piece is thirty-one minutes long, which is a bit of a commitment on your phone lines but the RealVideo options they give you are for both a 28.8 or 56K modem. Obviously the faster your modem, the better off you are, but what's really nice about the piece is that there isn't a lot of unnecessary action. One of the pitfalls of streaming video right now, due to the slowness of modems on analog phone lines, is that the effect of quick movements is lost because modems only show a few frames per second. At the beginning of this piece, the dancer almost seems aware of the limitations of the medium and takes it nice and slow.

The second piece on the "Features" page is an article on dance films by Belgian filmmaker Clara van Gool. There's also a

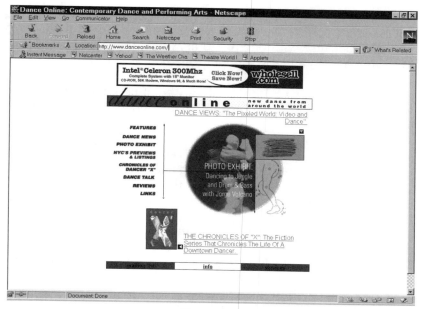

Figure 11-1

clip of one of the films. This piece requires downloading, so the quality of image is greater than streaming video but it takes time to download it. If you own a 56K modem each clip should only take a couple of minutes to download.

The next link on the home page is "Dance News." This column is published whenever there are interesting developments in the world of dance. In tandem on this same page is a column entitled "Dance Views." When I looked at the site the most recent dance view was an article titled "The Pixeled World: Video and Dance" by Clarinda MacLow, covering the connections between dance and technology—a connection that is quite eloqently expressed by the existence of this site. The left frame of this page contains links to past articles in "Dance Views," such as "Dollar Daze: Corporate Funding and The Arts."

"Photo Exhibit" is a series of dance photographs by Anja Hitzenberg. It's set up like a gallery, as if you're walking down a museum hall looking picture by picture, reading the little descriptions on the wall next to the pictures. Each page in this part of the site contains one picture and description, with a link below that will take you to the next page. One is an exploration of *Yves Musard's latest show on site at the Con Edison Building on 14th*

Street in NYC. The other is a series photographs from Andrea Mills' recent performance, "Elegant Strain." All these pages are fantastic, because with one photo per page, they don't take long to download. It's all very well put together.

"NYC's Previews & Listings" is a constantly updated listing of dance shows in New York City. It may be of no interest to people who aren't in New York, but it's always good to know what's going on!

"Chronicles of Dancer X" is another interesting page on the site. It is the serialized adventures of Dancer "X." It's fiction, written in the short-story form, that appears periodically in short installments. As of this writing, there were fifty-one little episodes. As a layman who's never been exposed to dance, I found this interesting to read.

There is also a section titled "Dance Talk" that features message boards covering several subject areas within the realm of dance. And, of course, there's a links page for other dance sites.

Overall, this is an outstanding site, ambitious in its use of video and also ambitious merely for its use of fiction in the context of discussing contemporary dance. A lot of Web sites merely exist as didactic storehouses of information but the makers of this site appear to have really put a lot of thought into approaching this site as something that can entertain as well as inform.

THE DANCE THEATRE SHOP
http://www.dancewear.com/nudts/index.html

This Web site opens with a spacescape like the one you see at the beginning of *Star Wars.* I'm not sure why, but regardless of how this site opens, it has nothing to do with space. It's a place where you can buy dance clothing online using the shopping cart form of online commerce.

The site is divided into sections devoted to footwear and bodywear. Once you select a section the site becomes a series of frames. I selected footwear. The left frame had a selection of links to types of footwear. I selected pointe for shoe type and a chart came up allowing me to select by gender/age categories—women or children in the case of the pointe shoes—and by manufacturer. After making a selection on the chart, I was connected to a page where I could click on "order" to add the shoes to my shopping cart. Then I could continue shopping and adding to and removing from my cart at will until I was ready to make the order.

Unfortunately, when I saw this site, there was no option for a secure server. However, you can also choose the "phone order" that which you can print out and use to order by phone or fax.

GAYNOR MINDEN, INC.
http://www.dancer.com

This is a very well-designed Web site by a manufacturer of pointe shoes. There's a page explaining the history of the product as well as a list of companies whose dancers wear it. There's a large FAQ page that answers questions I never even knew to ask. There's a page of testimonials, a page with excerpts from an article entitled "A Comparative Mechanical Analysis of the Pointe Shoe Toe Box: An In Vitro Study," and information on pricing.

DANCER ONLINE
http://www.danceronline.com

This great site is brought to you by the same people who bring you Dancer Newspaper. The site is made up of four components: Dancer Links, Dancer Mall, The Online Edition, and Competition Central.

Dancer Links is a page devoted to hundreds of dance-oriented links all over the Web. Running along the bottom of the Dancer Links page are buttons with subjects like Education, People, Research, and more that take you to lengthy links pages. You could spend days on Dancer Links. If you're someone who's really interested in finding all you can on dance on the Web, it's the most definitive guide to dance on the Web that I've been able to find and is an invaluable resource if you can't live without having quick access to as many dance sites as possible.

Dancer Mall is a series of online dance shops that begins with an exterior graphic of the "mall." You then have to navigate through several pages to finally get to a point where you shop. First you see the page with a map of the fake mall, then a page showing the exterior of a fake shop . . . it's all well and good to attempt to simulate reality by having visitors "stroll" through an online mall, but the Internet is supposed to be fast and I just want to get to my destination as quickly as possible. But once I did reach one of the two shops that were running when I accessed this site—Discount Dance Supply—I did find an online catalog that enabled me to order dance supplies online. It had a food selection and touted itself as giving you savings of up to thirty percent. This site uses the shopping cart format but, like The Dance Theatre Shop, does not have a secure server where you can safely enter credit card data.

The Online Edition doesn't give you much at all except information on how to subscribe to the newspaper and how to advertise in it. Then Competition Central touts itself as "THE major source of news and information on performing arts dance competitions for children and young adults in the United States." It's useful if you have a son or daughter in competition and wish to know where the competitions are. This part of the site is not as user-friendly as other parts. When I tried the first link, The Competition and Convention Calendar, it went to a page that offered a new link to that page and then a blank page—hopefully a temporary problem.

Overall, while not as impressive as Dance Online, Dancer Online is especially interesting as an online shopping option for dancers.

And, of course, there are many other interesting sites for dancers but I'll quit while I'm ahead and look at the world of the techie now.

Stagecraft 12

*I*t's important for the actor to be familiar with all parts of theatre and performance. The lights, the costumes, the direction . . . all are essential parts of your performance and you cannot just walk through your performing life not knowing what it is the techies do.

After all, you never know what you're going to be called upon to do in your acting career. You might think it's a good idea to learn about applying make-up, finding your light, or telling the difference between upstage and downstage. You might also want to look into directing and producing. This gets you into further details such as buying supplies for your theatre and yourself.

You'll want to think about costumes, props, and all the other necessary but sometimes mundane accoutrements that make your theatrical experiences possible. When you're acting on film you are often a slave to all the different pieces of equipment that point in your direction. You still should know what makes up a setup for film and commercials if you want to be wise about acting on film. So you might want to look for Web sites that explain the equipment being used.

Here I'll describe a few sites that can help you backstage at a theatre.

E-STAGE
http://www.estage.com

This site bills itself as "the online resource for backstages across the United States." It started out as a message board on America Online called "Backstage and Beyond." Besides the forum and message board, this site was devoid of any content when I looked at it, but it appeared to be under construction, so it's worth a look or two in the future. Given how quickly things change online, it could still be empty or incredibly comprehensive by the time you read this.

LIGHTING RELATED WWW SITES
http://www.mmsl.com/related.html

This is a simple page with a sickeningly bright yellow background, featuring dozens of links to Web pages for lighting resources. It's fairly comprehensive and much easier to use for this type of search than a regular search engine or directory.

CREW NET
http://www.crew-net.com

This site is a "casting call" for crew members for film, television, and stage. If you have production experience, you can join this site and post your resume for what it says is less than $1 a day, although the total price is mysteriously omitted.

NEW YORK DRAMA LEAGUE
http://mosaic.echonyc.com/~dlny/

This Web site opens with a front page that proclaims that "for over 80 years, **the Drama League** has been dedicated to strengthening the connection between artists and audiences, and to ensuring a vital, productive, and discerning theatre community. We have the history behind us—now join us, and make our experience . . . yours." The site also features a page detailing how to become a member of the league and the benefits of different giving levels ranging from $75 to $2,500.

Also featured is information on the Drama League Directors Project, which was founded in 1984. It is intended as a pathway to a successful career for young directors. There's a page detailing standards of eligibility and also an application to become a part of the Directors Project, which you have to download, print out, and mail for submission. There' was no online form available as of this writing. There is also a page giving updates on Directors Project alumni.

THE COSTUME SOCIETY OF AMERICA
http://www.costumesocietyamerica.com/

The Costume Society of America also is the first organization I've seen that actually has a form that allows you to sign up for or renew membership online with a credit card. You can reach this particular part of the site by clicking on the "Membership" link on the home page. The page explains how you can become a member just by having an interest in costume and receive the quarterly copy of CSA News and annual copy of Dress, the Journal of the Costume Society of America. The online application is on a secure server, and memberships start at $60 with different levels of benefits based on amount given. You can buy copies of the aforementioned Dress online as well, from a page that you can access from the home page.

There are also pages with information on regional symposia and the national symposium, a page devoted to information on awards and scholarships, and one containing a calendar of events. For those of you interested at all in costume, this is not a good site for straightforward information. It lacks the history, for example, of the Costume Society. But with a secure server for online purchases, it can get you products fairly quickly.

INTERNATIONAL COSTUMERS' GUILD
http://www.costume.org

This site's home page describes the International Costumers' Guild as " a worldwide organization of costume professionals and hobbyists chartered to promote the educational, cultural, literary, artistic, and theatrical advancement of costume design and construction..." and "promote public goodwill towards the costuming community . . ." by providing ". . . a public forum for the discussion of costume, clothing, and other related subjects through publications, conferences, and other special projects."

When I looked at the site, it offered links on the home page to more information on the "International Customers' Guild." Rule number one of making your own Web site is to spell the name of your organization correctly on your home page. Still, aside from that faux pas, this is a fairly decent Web site with plenty of details on this organization and upcoming events. It's updated regularly and even offers a report on the organization's annual meeting. Without much flash, this site provides information in a succinct manner and is another place to look if you're interested in becoming more active in costume.

DIGITAL THEATRE
http://www.theatresoftware.com

This is a site for "time management software." There are four links on the home page, the first of which is for the World Theatre Directory. The other three links cover "Products," "Ordering," and "News."

The "Products" page promotes three different pieces of software as "the only completely integrated solution available for tracking and managing production information on both the Macintosh and PC platforms." They are Virtual Cue Sheets, Virtual Theatre Forms, and Virtual Stage Management. A page with detailed information is devored to each product and there's also a pricing page. Each piece of software runs in the hundreds of dollars so it would be wise to do some further research beyond this site. There are no testimonials on this site.

The "Ordering" page instructs the user to click on a product to order but that portion of the site was not running as of this writing. The "News" page just details another pricing option on the software.

The real highlight of the site is "ShowNews."

GLOSSARY OF TECHNICAL THEATRE TERMS
http://www.ex.ac.uk/drama/tech/glossary.html

This is a great site based out of England. The glossary was compiled by Jon Primrose of the University of Exeter theatre department. He does note that although the site is based out of the England, comparable U.S. terms are included as well. There are two ways you can view the glossary: alphabetically or by category.

The glossary is comprehensive despite small differences in terminology. After all, theatre is theatre. Some entries say that they've becoming obsolete, as well as explain their origin.

Because this is obviously a text-heavy site you can either save the Web pages covering the glossary as a file on your hard disk that you can access and save as a document in your word processing program or you can download the Zip file rather than returning to the Web site again and again.

THE LIGHTING RESOURCE

http://www.lightresource.com

This site is intended to be a resource for lighting information for the theatre. One strike against this site when I looked at it was the banner on the home page announced the series of links along the bottom of the page as the index for the week of November 30, 1998. I looked at this page on February 3, 1999.

13 Other Actors Resources

*U*nder the umbrella of actors resources I've placed those sites that don't fit into one or another specific category like casting or education site. I'm going to tell you about some rather ambitious sites that you'll most likely turn to time and again. Created to exist as resources for actors, each site carries all kinds of information, from detailed links pages to audition notices. The parties responsible for the following sites run the gamut from large companies to individuals who saw a need for a site for actors and tried to fill it. All they needed was access to information and the desire to pass it along.

Several individual actors and big companies have Web sites that offer themselves as complete resources and are specifically geared toward casting or training. They are Web sites that provide news, and links to numerous other acting Web pages and essentially exist as search engines and directories for actors only. Most of these sites are storehouses of information and are updated quite often, with tender loving care. Given the constant changes that this industry goes through, a well-updated Web site is incredibly important. If you see a Web site that promises news and says it was last updated in 1994, you probably shouldn't waste your time checking it. That happens more often than you'd think. Sometimes pages that are never updated stay on the Web for years simply because the Webmaster forgot to delete it.

But you can avoid that by reading what's next. These sites are probably the first Web sites you want to look at once you're really immersed in your career and *especially* if you're in L.A. or New York.

1501BROADWAY.COM
http://www.geocities.com/~trenews/

This large Web site boasts many smaller Web sites underneath its vast storehouse of information. It is an intimidatingly large Web site with a home page that has a rather confusing interface with many small logos that connect you to different sections of the Web site. The home page has one cool feature, however: a ticker with updated theatre news.

The following are some fantastic resources on this site.

TRE E-Zine
http://www.geocities.com/~trenews/minis/tre.htm

This e-zine (online magazine) proclaims itself as "the magazine of theatre news, opinion, humor and trivia." Regular columns include Techie's Corner. In the edition that was online in January 1999 columnist Michael Powers went into detail about how to get water on stage, specifically water in sinks on stage. There's a "News and Gossip" section that's updated very regularly. There are several other articles on theatre personalities as well as a guide to theatre Web rings around the country. Web rings are "connected" Web sites that each have links to one another.

Virtual Broadway
http://www.geocities.com/~trenews/vbintro.htm

This part of the site looks like a large Broadway cityscape and a virtual walk through Broadway to connect to different show sites. It's a little hard to figure out, but once you get in, you're provided with a virtual map and directions to walk through and click on theatres on Broadway. It's worth a look.

Forum
http://www.geocities.com/~trenews/forum.htm

In this section of the site, you can post to different bulletin boards where you can discuss general theatre information or Shake-

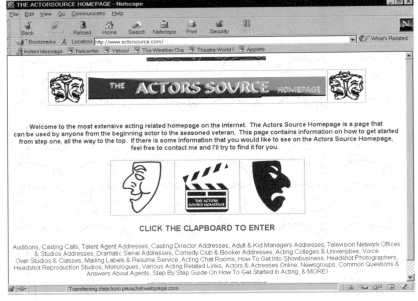

Figure 13–1

speare and the classics. There are also chat rooms but as with most realtime chat rooms the chance of finding someone else in there is pretty small.

THE ACTORSOURCE HOMEPAGE
http://www.actorsource.com

The Actorsource Homepage is an impressive Web site. It begins innocently enough on its home page, with a clapboard you click on in order to enter the site. It's a vast cornucopia of links to other sections of the Web site. The site is has a simple layout with nothing but the masks of tragedy and comedy guiding you (see Figure 13–1). At the top of the page is a menu of resources ranging from talent agent addresses to kids manager addresses. It does make a point of letting you know the listing of agents, etc. is not meant as an endorsement.

Next to the resources menu is a link for an actors survey. Next to that is a link to "Services," which takes you to a page full of informational essays. One essay is "An Actor's Headshot," a well-written basic list of rules to approaching your headshots Here's an excerpt from this particular essay:

White Clothes If you are having your photo session done indoors, then you might *not* want to wear white. My personal photographer told me this when I went for my photo session. White clothes can drain out your face too much and take too much attention away from your facial features. A white shirt with an darker overshirt or a jacket that is unbuttoned is ok though.

Dark Clothes Wearing a dark shirt is a good idea. A dark shirt can do the opposite of a white shirt as a dark shirt can draw your face into the "lookers" eyes more. A dark shirt will make your facial features stand out as it is a focal point.

Dark Clothes, Scruffy Look (for men) A set of dark clothes will again make your facial features stand out. For example, a leather jacket, t-shirt & slight beard growth is a good look if you are interested in getting into soap operas & film. It has the "Hollywood hunk" look.

Another informative essay is "Scams Used On Actors." This is full of links to pages detailing scams used against performers. An example comes from the Federal Trade Commission warning against

ads in newspapers [placed] to encourage potential models, both men and women, to interview with the agency. Many of the ads stated "No fee." However, the models who were "selected" by these agencies were asked to sign a contract agreeing to pay several hundred dollars for classes or photographs that the agency required before they could work as models.

The "Services" section of the Actorsource Homepage is full of little gems like this that are designed to help the actor.

The Actorsource Homepage also contains a links page that connects you to dozens of other acting-related Web sites. There's a page of questions and answers about agents, taken from the AFTRA home page. There's also a short essay called "How to Choose a Monologue," which isn't nearly as interesting or informative as other parts of the site but still offers some helpful advice.

You can also sign up to get e-mail notification of page updates.

ONSTAGE—THE ACTOR'S RESOURCE
http://www.onstage.org

This site is geared toward actors in New York and L.A., with many of the resources available on this site split into specific sections for one or the other city. As stated on the "How to Use" page, OnStage is "is an index to all of the theatrical production companies and performer support services that currently have a presence on the World Wide Web. If it has a website, you'll find it here."

The first link in the index goes to the "Theatre" section. The "Theatre" page has a search map that allows you to search for Web site of theatre companies in specific regions or states. The top of the page gives you the option of Chicago, New York, Los Angeles, or San Francisco. You also have the option of clicking on a state. To try out the database, I clicked on Chicago and retrieved about seventy-five links to theatre company sites. Some of the sites were more Chicago-specific than others and there were a couple of notable omissions but the links page was fairly comprehensive.

The "Auditions" page, at the time, was a rather disappointingly short list of links to casting sites, far fewer sites than really exist in that field. The "Services" page "lists photographers, photo and resume reproduction services, studios for rent, and other performer support services located in the New York and tristate area." The "Training" page is a series of training links specific to the New York and tristate area. And of course there is a regular "Links" page that lists links that don't fit into more specific categories.

There are plenty of Web sites out there for actors that simply function as pages of links to multiple acting Web sites. A book like this can't possibly go into detail on every Web site for actors but there is a vast number of actors' personal home pages and training pages out there to be discovered. The following pages are good reference guides to find more of what you want on the Web.

THEATRE CENTRAL
http://www.playbill.com/cgi-bin/plb/central?cmd=start

The URL above actually forwards to the Theatre Central portion of the Playbill Web site. Theatre Central used to be an independent site but as it has for years, it still boasts that it has "the largest compendium of theatre links on the Internet." The links cover everything from celebrity sites to dance sites to London theatre to stagecraft . . . it's a hard list to match.

ACTING RESOURCES FROM NERDWORLD MEDIA
http://www.nerdworld.com/nw884.html

As part of a larger site, this series of links to different acting-related Web sites lists them alphabetically, ranging from individual training centers to other links pages to actors' personal home pages.

Of course, each of these two sites' links have links to other pages, and those have links to other pages. Don't limit yourselves to just the sites you see in this book. Remember there will always be new sites on the Web and the next chapter will tell you how to make one of your own.

14 Building Your Very Own Web Site

Now that you've gotten online and looked at a variety of Web sites, you may have noticed there are some subject matters that aren't covered by the sites you've visited. For example, I discovered no one had created a Web page devoted to silent film stars Douglas Fairbanks and Mary Pickford. At least, I couldn't find one. So I decided to start a page myself. The isn't particularly complicated but it exists as a resource for anyone who wants to learn about these stars.

You may be part of a theatre company or organization and think it would help your company or organization to have a presence on the Internet. Don't feel bad if you don't already. The mighty Actors' Equity didn't have a site up until the end of 1998, and it probably has more resources and money than you to produce a really top-notch Web site. It's becoming a rule, however, for any business to market itself in some capacity on the Internet.

On the other hand, you might just want a personal Web page to promote yourself. However, be advised that if online casting pages' success rate is questionable, personal home pages' success rates for winning you roles is even more so. A personal Web page can simply exist as another source of contact for you, like your phone number, fax number, pager number, cell phone number, and e-mail address.

Before you begin programming your Web page, you have to learn how to do it, what software to use, and other intricate design rules that exist on the Web. Fortunately, basic Web programming is shockingly easy. With just a few keystrokes you can have a Web page that—while not visually stunning—will be accessible to the same millions of people who rush to Netscape Netcenter every day.

You should begin by to learning the programming language that is the foundation of the World Wide Web: HTML.

Discovering HTML

HTML stands for "hypertext markup language." It defines the purpose of the Web. At its most basic, the Web is simply a series of pages that are accessible through hyperlinks, those words that are often highlighted andunderlined. As I stated earlier, the software used to view Web pages is known as browsers. When you enter the address of a Web page, you're essentially sending instructions to a given server to open that page. Then the HTML file sends instructions to your browser defining how the Web page should look to the viewer.

There are quite a few Web pages that offer online instruction on HTML, but you don't want to get caught learning advanced material before you get to the beginners material. While HTML is easy to learn, there are still definite steps you have to take before you can get to more advanced features like tables and forms.

NCSA—A BEGINNER'S GUIDE TO HTML
http://www.ncsa.uiuc.edu/General/Internet/WWW/HTMLPrimer.html

This site is a great primer for those of you who wouldn't know HTML from a hole in the wall. It's a very simple lesson that gets you familiar with some of the basics of the language. It tells you how to create the building blocks of Web pages, those HTML instructions that must be there in order for a Web page to even be recognized as an HTML document, and it gives other basic instructions on HTML.

THE BARE BONES GUIDE TO HTML
http://werbach.com/barebones/

This guide is updated frequently to go along with the new versions of HTML that come out. Just three days before I checked out this site, Version 4.0 of the guide became available to conform with HTML 4.0. You can download the guide in twenty-one different languages. It's a valuable online resource for learning everything you can about HTML. This isn't so much geared toward beginners, but there's a lot of good material and it's great if you don't want to lug an instructional book around with you.

If you do want to lug an instructional book around, there are dozens to choose from. It is often best to learn the latest edition of HTML. The following are some of the books that teach HTML:

> *Teach Yourself Web Publishing with HTML4 in a Week* by Laura Lemay (Sams, 1997)
> *HTML Publishing for Netscape* by Gayle Kidder and Stuart Harris (Ventura Press, 1997)

These happen to be the books I own and have found useful. If you go to your local bookstore and check out the computers and business sections, you will likely see rows and rows of HTML instruction books.

Choosing an HTML Editor

In order to program HTML, you don't need fancy software. All you need is a text editor. A text editor is basically a bare-bones word processor without choices for fonts or anything. For example, the text editor in Windows is Notepad.

When you learn HTML, you'll learn that "tags" make up the instruction portion of the language. These tags surround the actual text you want to appear on the page. For example, when you want a piece of text on the Web page to be bold face you must place tags around it:

    This is a sentence in boldface.

The first tag tells the Web browser that the following text will be bold. The second tag lets the browser know that the boldface portion should end at that point.

The problem with using a simple text editor to program your HTML is a matter of time consumption. You don't really want to type those tags again and again. So, in order to save you time, the HTML editor was invented. An HTML editor can simply provide shortcut buttons for certain tags, or it can be something as complex as Microsoft Front Page or Macromedia Dreamweaver that enables you to build a Web page in a WYSIWYG—what you see is what you get—fashion, without typing any HTML tags at all.

There are quite a few HTML editors that you can download as either freeware or shareware. Freeware is simply software that you can download for free and use as much as you like. Shareware is also often free, but it only will function for a specific period of time, often advising you at the end of that time that you need to purchase a licensed version in order to keep using it. Much shareware gives you the option of making the purchase online via credit card, at which point your software magically begins working again.

Regardless of whether you download shareware or purchase an editor in a box at a store how much you want to spend on an HTML editor depends on how serious you are about producing a really sophisticated Web site. If your Web site is going to be something simple, with just text and a picture or two, that you won't update that often, you would be better off spending as little as possible. It isn't worth it to spend $100 or more on a high-end editor unless you're really interested in updating a site frequently and featuring a lot of pages within the site.

HOT DOG PROFESSIONAL
http://www.sausage.com

This shareware editor is available for trial for thirty days. One of the better known of the old HTML editors, the new version, 5.1 professional, lets you see what your Web page will look like as you program it in HTML. After thirty days you need to purchase a "key" (password) in order to keep using the software. The last time I looked, the key cost about $200.

MACROMEDIA DREAMWEAVER
http://www.macromedia.com/software/dreamweaver/trial/

This editor also gives you the capability to view the Web page as you type in HTML instructions. You can also type and insert images in the window itself. This download also contains a thirty-day trial package that you can then purchase electronically for $269.

MICROSOFT FRONT PAGE
http://www.microsoft.com/frontpage

This software is a great time-saver, geared toward people who don't want to deal with HTML at all. Front Page works much like a word processing program like Microsoft Word, in that all you have to do to build a Web page is simply type into the Web page and insert images. More advanced functions are also given short-cuts, enabling the user to avoid having to type in the HTML code. The program types the HTML code as you type "normal" words in the window.

If you want to enter HTML code yourself for any reason, you can hit "View HTML" to see exactly what the program has put in as HTML code and you can add any code you like to it.

Unfortunately, Front Page is much too large to download with your normal 56K modem, so you have to get out of chair in order to get it. It retails for about $150, usually giving you the option to send in for a rebate.

ADOBE PAGE MILL
http://www.adobe.com/prodindex/pagemill/main.html

This software also allows you to view the Web page while you type HTML commands or simply insert text and images into a window as if it were a word processor. You can download both Power Mac and PC versions of this editor. They are shareware versions; the Mac version lasts thirty days and the Windows version lasts 15 days. You can simply buy it and then download it for $79.

These four are not the only HTML editors out there worth looking at. I mentioned these because they're about as sophisticated as you're going to get and they let you see how the Web page will appear as you build it. There are plenty more HTML editors that cost less money but they also have fewer features.

Following the Rules

No matter what kind of HTML editor you use there are some important rules you have to consider even if you're only building a simple one-page Web site.

HYPERLINKS

Make sure any hyperlinks you include on a Web site are up to date. If a user clicks on a "broken link"—one that doesn't go any-where—said user will most likely abandon your site.

Also, if you have a site with multiple pages, you should give the user an easy way to link back to any page on the site no mat-ter which page he or she happens to be on at the moment.

The ImprovOlympic Web site from Chicago is an example of a good way to ensure that the user can link to any part of the site (see Figure 14–1). Many of the sites mentioned in this volume fea-ture the same kind of menu bar that runs along the left side of this site's Web pages. The menu bar exists on every page so visitors can quickly switch from one page to another.

IMAGES

You'll find that some graphics files take up more memory than others once you get started. A small line drawing in black and white may take up 1K, which would take most modems less than a second to download, and a large color photograph can take up 100K, which would take modems at least 30 seconds to down-load. You don't want a bunch of 100K images on your Web page, because modems must download images one at a time. Be nice to your users. What really matters on your site is content. That means text, and that doesn't take very long to download at all.

PLUG-INS

If you want to get more advanced you can add features to your page that require users to download plug-ins in order to view them correctly. It is not a good idea to have a site with more than one or two plug-in features because you don't want to force your visitors to spend all their time downloading plug-ins just so they can see your Web site.

Creating a Personal Home Page

There are an infinite number of things you can do with your Web site. One option is to create an actor's personal home page.

If you are really interested in having your own personal home page, you want to look at it realistically. When you read about casting Web sites, you probably noticed it's a big hit-or-miss proposition, especially as the industry tries to finds its footing and figure out the proper role of the Internet in casting. The personal home page is even more of a risk. But does this mean you won't get noticed? No. Take the following personal home page, for example.

CARYN.COM
http://www.caryn.com

One of the more outstanding Web sites for an actor is this site from Caryn Shalita. It is a resource page as well as a page where she can promote herself. It is much more ambitious than the average home page and has quite a few resources that any actor would find useful. Other Web sites link to this page. If you want to have a personal home page, you have to promote yourself through a site that regular people with an interest in the acting profession are going to visit.

AIN'T IT COOL NEWS
http://www.aint-it-cool-news.com

This non-acting-related site was started by Harry Knowles in Austin, Texas, and has made him world-famous. He employs a collection of "spies" that get scoops on upcoming films and have helped him become very influential in Hollywood. Audience members who see special preview screening post reviews as does he. He gets invited to all the film festivals because of the power he wields on the Internet. He even got a guest appearance on Siskel & Ebert.

Could a lowly actor achieve this kind of attention? Of course. It's going to involve a heck of a lot of work, but a heck of a lot of work is the only chance you have of getting a whole lot of recognition.

Thus, you have two choices. You can simply post you resume and headshot on the Web, impressing your friends and relatives, or you can devote yourself to a site that you believe will garner you a lot of attention.

CONTENT

This is the most important component of your Web page. You can learn all you like about RealAudio, Animated Graphics, and Javascript, but if you have nothing to say on your page it doesn't mean a thing.

In early 1997 I began a Web site I called "Impravda-Improv Truth." I am part of the rather unique Chicago improv community that consists of Second City, ImprovOlympic, The Annoyance

Theatre, and a handful of other theatres that devote themselves to improvisational theatre. One of the existing improv-related Web sites had not been updated for quite some time, so I thought there was an opening for someone to offer improv theatre listings and news for Web readers.

I also saw a possibility to satirize the gossip that runs through any community of any size and type, run articles about the art of improvisation, and offer links to other improv and theatre Web sites.

Then I began to promote my page through word of mouth and by hanging posters with the URL in improv theatres. I garnered more attention for my page than any amount of stage time I got in any of the improv theatres. I started to get as many as fifty hits, or visits, a day on the Web site.

If you want to be noticed on a large scale, find something that isn't addressed at all on the web or something that isn't addressed well enough and create a site that fills the void.

MAINTENANCE

You must always check your Web page to make sure it's active. An easy way to do this is to simply make it the default home page in your browser, meaning it will appear every time you open your browser. The traffic on analog phone lines caused by the incredible growth of users of the Internet has taxed many Internet service providers as far as they can go. Please make sure your home page is working. Also , even if you're not updating your page's actual contents, it's sometimes a good idea simply to update the date on the page so at least the viewer knows you still work on the page periodically.

It's important to keep information current. While updating your print resume can be a hassle in terms of printing costs and attaching new headshots, all you have to do on the Web is type a few words, upload, and you're done. It takes only a few minutes to do so.

Creating a Theatre Company Home Page

Let's say you are a founding member of the Whammo Theatre Company and you want your company to have its own Web site.

When your theatre company takes on the grueling ordeal of

ιɛgιstering with an Internet service provider, it is almost always worth it to register your theatre company's name as the domain name. If your Whammo Theatre Company is a nonprofit, your Web page address could be "whammo.org"; if it is a for-profit the name could be "whammo.com."

Logical domain names make searching for Web sites so much easier. If John Q. Public is looking for Whammo Theatre Company on the Web, he might automatically type "whammo.com" in the hope that your site will appear. Although the $70 investment for brand awareness on the Internet for an actor's personal home page isn't really worth it, is absolutely mandatory for any kind of business. However, with a domain name comes higher expenses at your internet service provider. It has to create a special folder on its server just for your domain name and it will likely charge you for this service. The lowest ISP price for domain name service and Web hosting I've seen is from ConcentricHost, a national company. The downside to the service is that unless you live near its California offices, you're on hold for as long as half an hour. Often your best bet is to use a local ISP—there's a much better chance of forming a personal relationship, which is often helpful.

After you figure out which HTML editor to use, you should remember one thing: the Web provides you with a platform that gives you the opportunity to go beyond mere advertising—you can build a site that reflects your company in an entertaining way.

CONTENT

When creating a theatre company home page, you have much more to deal with than the promotion of a single actor. Thus, rather than letting your own personality show too much, you become more of a hired hand, promoting a whole organization's image and product. There is also precious little time to waste. So if you're going to spend any time at all on a Web site, make sure it's good. You want to give the Whammo Theatre Company name recognition and you want to make the home page an attraction in itself.

The following are a few suggestions places to places to start when planning your content:

- Give all the basic information on your company and then expand on it.
- Create an archive of your company.
- Create articles as your shows are produced.
- Create interactivity.

You must never create a web page simply because you feel *obligated* to, simply because every other theatre company in your city has already done so. Rust and doom will result. You should take this wonderful tool and exploit it in every way you can. By now you have reviewed some theatre company Web sites and are surely surprised at the lack of imagination many of them exhibit. The webmasters have confined their creativity to the stage. If you allow yourself to do that, you shouldn't bother putting a page on the Web. Just as with every other medium, there is so much out there that is completely dull that really putting some thought and heart into your page, will gain quite a bit more attention for your company.

Give all the basic information on your company and then expand on it. This starts out being easy. It is mandatory that you provide the list of upcoming shows and the mission of your company. Let your reader know who's in the ensemble, where the theatre is, and how to get tickets. Also, it's extremely important to give a history of your company. It seems pretty obvious to include all that information, but a lot of theatres decide to stop right there. To stand out you wnat to go above and beyond the basics. Let's say in the fall you're putting up *The Man Who Came to Dinner* by Kaufman and Hart. You might want to include an essay explaining why your company chose the show, detailing a history of the show, giving examples of some famous productions of the show, etc. Don't just stop with the title, author, and the dates it's running.

Also, in addition to providing address, phone number, and ticket information, you could show a seating chart of the theatre and provide a link to Yahoo! maps, which could show how to get to the theatre from a set destination.

Create an archive of your company. With all the memory available to you on the Web, you can also create a history for your theatre that patrons can navigate through. One of the disappointments I've had in looking at sites of theatre companies that have rich histories is a complete lack of pictures from earlier eras. I want to see photos of Gary Sinise in his first play, complete with remembrances. The founders of your company should dig through every photo of members of the company that exists. Even if your company has produced only one show, you can still form a sense of your history and show that you're truly accomplishing something. Some companies never make it that far. If nothing else, on those days that the balance in the account looks particularly low, you yourself can use the site as an affirmation of what you're trying to do.

Create articles as your shows are produced. This is a great way to involve your reader in the wonderful evolution of a real life theatrical production. One of the disadvantages to a dry web page containing just a compilation of lists is that a reader would only have to visit it once. By updating your page on a consistent basis with active content, you tempt the reader to come back. Also, you provide a valuable learning experience for those who are interested in the theatre production process as well.

There are, of course, several people who would be well-suited to provide a perspective on your Web page. The first that comes to mind, naturally, is the director of the show. He or she can first explain how the decision was made to do this particular show and what the director sees in the show. In writing this kind of commentary the director should answer some of these questions: What is the purpose of this show? Is the company doing it to make a political statement, or is this one of those safe revivals with name recognition that will guarantee bigger houses so the theatre can later afford to do plays with a riskier financial investment? What thought did the director put into casting? What is his or her primary vision of the set and lighting design? There are, of course, many directions you could go with this, but it should give you an idea of the freedom a Web site gives you to present pertinent information about your company.

Others who could provide show journals are cast members, those wonderful crazy techies, or peripheral members of the cast. Anyone associated with your production could write about the show. Although there's a danger that writers will air complaints and dirty laundry to the public, hopefully everyone will be savvy enough to know that the purpose of advertising is to show how wonderful you all are. With a behind-the-scenes guide to your productions, you provide an extra feature that will make people come *back* to your page and thus become more likely to want to see the shows.

Create interactivity. Interactivity has been the buzzword for some time now. With all the hubbub about Interactive TV and Virtual Reality games, the Internet has become the ultimate interactive tool. But even so, the Internet has a primarily one-way feel: it's a place where people can obtain all kinds of information, but not everyone feels that he or she is a part of the process. As modems and computers continue to get faster, a majority of computer owners will soon have newer browsers that allow people to use more interactive programs written in

Java and ActiveX, programming languages that allow for the creation of more sophisticated animation and forms.

To increase the interactiveness of your site to make visitors feel more involved, you might consider trying to sell tickets online if you have a credit card merchant account. However, if you're modestly sized, you might not be be able to afford putting that in motion. You will almost certainly need to hire an outside person to program a page for online purchases, since it really isn't time-effective to try to learn how to do the more complicated work yourself. And if you're a small theatre company, it isn't cost-effective either.

Another way to create interactivity is to create a chat room and schedule events when your artistic director, for example, will appear to answer questions. There are Web sites that will create chat rooms for other sites for free in exchange for a small advertising space at the bottom of the chat room. So while there's little chance more than one person will go into the room at a time unless you schedule an event, it's the right price and literally takes less than five minutes to complete. Forms and polls are good ways to get audience feedback since small slips of paper hauled out at shows often get misplaced of thrown to the wind.

MAINTENANCE

There's one simple rule: Never, never, *never* let your information become out dated. If your season is over, stop promoting it as "upcoming." I have seen so many theatre companies leave useless information one their sites after their seasons are over and the new ones have already been announced in the press. When a season ends, relegate all related information to your archives. Then start pushing the upcoming season with vigor, even for those plays that haven't been decided on yet.

Using Your Imagination

There are countless other ways to create a home page either for yourself or for an organization you represent. The Web is growing and changing at an astonishing rate. Pay attention to how other Web pages change. For example, the Chicago Tribune has changed its Web site so many times it makes the head spin. It has the resources to constantly change with the times, to update the functionality, and add new toys as another wave of faster modems makes it through the market, but you can always get ideas from watching what other web sites are doing with design and functionality.

The only mandatory rule in making your Web page is *never limit yourself.* The entire world has access to your information, whereas ten years ago only those you knew personally did. There are millions of people just a keystroke away from you—give them something to see.

Appendix 1: The Actor's Guide to URLs

Chapter 3: How to Get Online

Dell
http://www.dell.com

Gateway
http://www.gateway.com

Apple
http://www.apple.com

America Online
http://www.aol.com

CompuServe
http://www.compuserve.com

Prodigy
http://www.prodigy.com

CNET's Review of Internet Service Providers
http://www.cnet.com/Content/Reports/Special/ISP/index.html

The List—The Buyer's Guide to ISP's
http://thelist.internet.com

Netscape Communicator
http://www.netscape.com

Microsoft Internet Explorer
http://www.microsoft.com/ie

Opera
http://www.operasoftware.com

Lynx
http://www.lynx.browser.org
NeoPlanet
http://www.neoplanet.com
Eudora
http://www.eudora.com
Yahoo!
http://www.yahoo.com
Excite
http://www.excite.com
Hotmail
http://www.hotmail.com
Rocketmail
http://www.rocketmail.com

Chapter 4: E-Mail and Newsgroups

Netiquette Home Page
http://www.albion.com/netiquette/index.html
Improv Resource Center
http://www.sitepowerup.com/mb/view.asp?BoardID=102196
Deja News
http://www.dejanews.com
rec.arts.theatre.misc
rec.arts.theatre.stagecraft
alt.stagecraft
alt.comedy.improvisation
rec.arts.theatre.plays

Chapter 5: Search Engines and Directories

Netscape Netcenter
http://www.netscape.com
Internet Addiction
http://www.netaddiction.com
Yahoo!
http://www.yahoo.com

Look Smart
http://www.looksmart.com
Magellan Internet Guide
http://magellan.excite.com
Webcrawler
http://www.webcrawler.com
Snap
http://www.snap.com
CNET's Review of Search Engines
*http://www.cnet.com/Content/Reviews/Compare/Search2/
    ?st.cn.fd.accol.re*
Excite
http://www.excite.com
HotBot
http://www.hotbot.com
AltaVista
http://www.altavista.com
Infoseek
http://www.infoseek.com
Go
http://www.go.com
Ask Jeeves
http://www.askjeeves.com
Metacrawler
http://www.metacrawler.com
Dogpile
http://www.dogpile.com

Chapter 6: Education

Overview of Colleges, Vocational Schools and Careers
http://www.overview.com/colleges/index.html
Overview of College Financial Aid
http://www.overview.com/colleges/college-financial-aid.htm
College and University Home Pages—Alphabetical Listing
http://www.mit.edu/people/cdemello/univ.html
Embark.com
http://www.embark.com
CollegeNET
http://www.collegenet.com

Advanced Book Exchange
http://www.abebooks.com

The Internet Theatre Bookshop
http://ourworld.compuserve.com/homepages/paul_thain/abooks.htm

Samuel French
http://www.samuelfrench.com

Baker's Plays
http://www.bakersplays.com

Broadway Play Publishing, Inc.
http://www.broadwayplaypubl.com

Quite Specific Media
http://www.quitespecificmedia.com

Act I Bookstore
http://www.act1books.com

Stage & Screen Book Club
http://www.stagenscreen.com

An Annotated Bibliography of Commedia dell'Atre, Music Hall, Pantomine, and Other Diversions
http://www.214b.com

The Association of American University Presses Online Catalog
http://aaup.princeton.edu/

Textbook Club from Varsity Books
http://www.varsitybooks.com/textbookclub/index.asp

The On-Line Books Page
http://www.cs.cmu.edu/books.html

The Complete Works of William Shakespeare
http://www-tech.mit.edu/Shakespeare/works.html

BiblioBytes
http://www.bb.com

On-Line Script Showcase
http://www.newplays.com

The Dramatic Exchange: Catalog of Plays
http://www.dramex.org/htmlplays.html

The Online Scripthouse
http://webhome.idirect.com/~taggart5/scripthouse/ie4.htm

Script World
http://www.screenwriter.com/scriptworld.html

Chapter 9: Unions and Organizations

Actors' Equity Association
http://www.actorsequity.org

Screen Actors Guild
http://www.sag.com

SAG-PPHP Home Page
http://www.sagph.org/

AFTRA
http://www.aftra.org

Canadian Actors' Equity Association
http://www.caea.com/

AFL-CIO
http://www.aflcio.org

Chapter 10: Casting Online

The Film, TV and Commercial Employment Network
http://www.employnow.com

TalentWorks
http://www.talentworks.com

ShowBizJobs.com
http://www.showbizjobs.com

National Talent Pool
http://www.nationaltalent.com

TalentScene
http://www.talentscene.com

BuzzNYC/BuzzLA
http://www.buzznyc.com

Cast-A-Head
http://www.castahead.com

CastNet
http://www.castnet.com

Extracast
http://www.extracast.com

Academy of Motion Pictures Arts and Sciences Players Directory
http://www.acadpd.org

The Link
http://www.submitlink.com

Casting and Media On-Line, Inc. (CAMEO)
http://www.cameo.net

Chapter 11: Dance

Sapphire Swan Dance Directory
http://www.sapphireswan.com/dance/

Dance Online
http://www.danceonline.com

The Dance Theatre Shop
http://www.dancewear.com/nudts/index.html

Gaynor Minden, Inc.
http://www.dancer.com

Dancer Online
http://www.danceronline.com

Chapter 12: Stagecraft

E-Stage
http://www.estage.com

Lighting Related WWW Sites
http://www.mmsl.com/related.html

Crew Net
http://www.crew-net.com

New York Drama League
http://mosaic.echonyc.com/~dlny/

The Costume Society of America
http://www.costumesocietyamerica.com/

International Costumers' Guild
http://www.costume.org

Digital Theatre
http://www.theatresoftware.com

Glossary of Technical Theatre Terms
http://www.ex.ac.uk/drama/tech/glossary.html
The Lighting Resource
http://www.lightresource.com

Chapter 13: Other Actors Resources

1501Broadway.com
http://www.geocities.com/~trenews/
TRE E-Zine
http://www.geocities.com/~trenews/minis/tre.htm
Virtual Broadway
http://www.geocities.com/~trenews/vbintro.htm
Forum
http://www.geocities.com/~trenews/forum.htm
The Actorsource Homepage
http://www.actorsource.com
OnStage—The Actor's Resource
http://www.onstage.org
Theatre Central
http://www.playbill.com/cgi-bin/plb/central?cmd=start
Actors Resources from NerdWorld Media
http://www.nerdworld.com/nw884.html

Chapter 14: Building Your Very Own Web Page

NCSA—A Beginner's Guide to HTML
http://www.ncsa.uiuc.edu/General/Internet/WWW/HTMLPrimer.h tml
The Bare Bones Guide to HTML
http://werbach.com/barebones/
Hot Dog Professional
http://www.sausage.com
Macromedia Dreamweaver
http://www.macromedia.com/software/dreamweaver/trial/

Microsoft Front Page
http://www.microsoft.com/frontpage

Adobe PageMill
http://www.adobe.com/prodindex/pagemill/main.html

Appendix 2
The CD-ROM

The CD-ROM accompanying this volume is intended to get you going on the Internet.

CD-ROM Files

All files are on the enclosed Zip disk in the CD-ROM Files folder.

NETSCAPE COMMUNICATOR 4.5 FOR WINDOWS AND MACINTOSH

This popular Web browser will connect you to Heinemann Books' Internet Service Provider if you do not already have one and connect you immediately to the updated *Actor's Guide to the Internet* Web site located at *http://www.heinemann.com/actorsguide*.

And to download new versions of Netscape Communicator go to *http://www.netscape.com*.

WS_FTP 6.0

For Windows 95 and 98 users, WS_FTP is a file transfer protocol program that allows you to upload your Web site material to your ISP's FTP server.

This is a shareware evaluation version that will last you for thrity days. For more information on how to purchase a fully registered version of WS_FTP go to *http://www.ipswitch.com/ Products/WS_FTP/index.html.*

FETCH 3.03

For Macintosh users, WS_FTP is a file transfer protocol program that allows you to upload your Web site material to your ISP's FTP server.

WINZIP

* WinZip 7.0 evaluation for Windows 95/98
* WinZip 6.3 evaluation for Windows 3.1

This evaluation version of WinZip for Windows users will last for thirty days. WinZip allows you to open zip files, as well as create zip files. This compresses your files so they take up less of your precious disk space.

In order to purchase a full registered version of WinZip, visit the Web site at *http://www.winzip.com.*

ACTOR'S GUIDE TO URLS

This Web page is local and can be updated from the *Actor's Guide to the Internet* Web site.

Appendix 3
Glossary of Terms

applet: A computer program written in the Java language that lets you do incredible things on the Web.

archive: A single file that contains several compressed files in order to store them more easily. Also known as **Zip files** or **Stuffit files**.

attachment: A file that you can send over the Internet with an e-mail.

baud: The number of electrical symbols sent over the phone lines per second.

bcc: Blind carbon copy. Bcc addresses allow you to send e-mail to certain recipients without your other recipients ever knowing it.

bookmark: In Netscape Navigator, a bookmark is a saved Web page URL that you can simply click to get to that Web page rather than having to type the URL again and again.

bounce: A returning undeliverable message. These are e-mails sent to bad e-mail addresses that are then returned to you.

browser: Software that allows you to see Web pages.

byte: One character of data. For example, the words "One character of data" take up 22 bytes. Spaces are also considered characters of data.

cc: Carbon copy. Cc addressees get a copy of your e-mail. All Cc recipients see the other e-mail addresses the message went to, unlike Bcc.

channel: In IRC, this is a group of people chatting together. In America Online and CompuServe, these are called **chat rooms**.

chat: To talk live to other users on the Internet.

client: When you're on the Internet, your computer is called a client of the enormous network because you're receiving the services of another computer, which is called a **server**.

cookie: A text file that is stored on your computer when you access a Web site. When you visit the Web site again, the text file reminds the Web site that you're you and that you've been there before

Dial-Up Networking: The communications software that comes with Windows 95 and Windows 98 that allows you to dial up the Internet.

domain: The name that identifies a computer on the Internet. Some examples of domains are actorsequity.org and cast-net.com.

domain-name server: A computer on the Internet that translates URLs on the Web into the numerical addresses (like 206.126.224.1) that is the actual code with which computers on the Internet communicate. It's important to know your ISP's domain name servers so you can dial them up.

download: The transferring of files from a remote computer to your own computer.

e-mail: Mail sent electronically.

FAQ: Frequently asked questions. A time saving method that newsgroups and Web sites provide their users to answer specific questions that are often asked. Someone in a newsgroup will often post FAQs on a regular basis to keep everyone informed.

firewall: A computer that connects a local network to the Internet and only lets some information pass back and forth.

flame: A crime in the annals of Netiquette. To flame is to post angry, insulting, and generally ugly messages.

flame war: The result of two or more people flaming each other with great frequency and ferocity.

FTP: File transfer protocol. A method of transferring files from another computer to your computer and vice versa. You'll use an FTP program when you work on your own Web page, uploading files from your computer to your host server.

GIF: A graphics file format that is patented by CompuServe and used all over the Web because it's a small file size and quick to download. You will most likely use quite a few GIFs when you build a Web page.

gigabyte: One billion bytes. See **byte**.

Gopher: An Internet system older than the Web that you'll probably never encounter. It helps you find information by using menus. No pictures, just text.

gov: A domain-name extension, for example, www.loc.gov, that indicates the site is operated by a government organization, usually the federal government.

handle: The name a user on the Internet chooses as his or her screen name or nickname.

header: The entire beginning of an e-mail address that contains information on the sender, the receiver, the subject of the e-mail, often the date and time sent, and other Internet codes that make the e-mail get to its destination.

hierarchy: Usenet categories like "alt, "rec," etc.

home page: The first page you see when you visit a Web site. It can also refer to a person's or company's Web site.

HTML: Hypertext markup language. The programming language that forms the basis of Web pages. It contains instructions for Web browsers on how the site should appear.

HTTP: Hypertext transfer protocol. The "http://" starts the URL of every Web page. It's the method by which Web pages are transferred on the Internet.

HTTPS: The way that Web pages are transferred with encryption. You never type this in. It's something that appears once you enter a secure Web page.

hypertext: Text on a Web page that is "highlighted" and contains a link to another Web page or e-mail address or Usenet address.

Internet: A network linking millions of computers sharing information.

Internet Explorer: Microsoft's Web browser software.

InterNIC: The Internet Network Information Center. A central place on the Web for information on the Internet. If you build a Web site you can register for a unique domain name at its Web site at *http://www.internic.net*.

intranet: A network like the Internet but contained within private boundaries like that of a corporate office environment.

IRC: Internet relay chat. The Internet system that lets users communicate with each other instantaneously.

ISDN: Integrated Services Digital Network. Special digital phone lines that allow you to transfer information at a rate as high as 128K.

Java: A programming language developed by Sun Microsystems. On the Web, it's used as a platform for many purposes, such as changing graphics when you move a cursor over them, animations, scrolling marquees, etc.

JPEG: Joint Photographic Experts Group. Another graphics file format that is popular on the Web. Photo files in this format are much smaller and faster to download.

Kill file: This is a file in your newsreader that tells you which postings to skip.

kilobyte: One thousand bytes or 1K. See **byte**. (For computers, kilobyte often actually means 1,024 bytes which is two to the tenth power bytes.)

link: Something on a Web page that, when clicked, takes you to another Web page. Links can appear as text or graphics.

lurk: Reading newsgroups without posting any messages.

mail server: A server on the Internet that provides mail services.

mailbot: Automatic e-mail software.

mailing list: Akin to a subscription to a regular e-mail from a source. Mailing lists are often in the form of newsletters.

megabyte: A million bytes. See **byte**.

mirror: An FTP server or Web page that provides the same files as another site. You'll often see "mirror sites" for very popular Web sites that get hevy traffic.

modem: The hardware that is connected to your phone line or cable and to your computer that allows your computer to connect with other computers.

moderator: A person who looks at messages in a newsgroup or message board and removes those that are offensive or off-topic.

MP3: A downloadable audio file that has a very small file size but has compact disc quality.

MPEG: Moving picture experts group. This is a downloadable video file that is often used on the Web.

net: Short for network, or in this context, the Internet.

network computer: A computer with no hard disk that gets all data from a network and/or the Internet.

newbie: A newcomer to the Internet.

news server: A computer on the Internet that provides access to Usenet.

newsgroup: A place where Internet users congregate to post messages regarding a specific subject.

newsreader: Software that allows you to access newsgroups and post messages to them.

nickname: Screen name or handle by which you identify yourself on the Internet.

org: A domain-name extension, for example, actorsequity.org, for a non-profit organization.

page: A document on the World Wide Web that you can read with a Web browser.

password: A secret word that only you know to access information on Web sites.

plug-in: A piece of software you can often download that you add to your Web browser to help it read special files on Web pages.

POP or POP3: Post office protocol. The way your computer communicates with your mail server to download e-mail.

push: A kind of program, or technology, that allows you to receive information automatically from the Web without asking for it every time.

QuickTime: A video file format from Apple that is downloadable.

RealAudio: An audio file format that "streams," meaning you don't have to wait to listen to it until after you download it. You listen to it while it comes through your modem.

router: A computer that connects two or more networks.

RTFM: Read the —— Manual. A reply code in newsgroups and message boards used when someone asks a question that can be easily answered elsewhere.

search engine: A Web site that uses software called "spiders" to search through millions of Web pages to find keywords you enter in order to find pages that fit as closely as possible to your search parameters.

secure server: A computer that provides encrypted Web pages, messages, etc. that make it supremely difficult for someone else to take a look. Always make sure you're on a secure server before entering potentially dangerous information such as your credit card number.

server: A computer that provides data that you can retrieve on your computer.

shareware: Software that you can download but must pay for in order to keep. You're often given a thirty-day trial period before it stops functioning unless you pay for it, usually online.

Shockwave: One of the most popular plug-ins, from Macromedia, that lets you see various multimedia on the Web.

SMTP: Simple mail transfer protocol. This is the way computers send e-mail to each other. In your e-mail program, you need to know what your SMTP server is in order to send e-mail. It's almost always the same server as the dial-up ISP you're using.

spam: E-mail sent to many people at once, usually to sell something. The practice is considered poor Netiquette.

streaming audio: Audio software that allows you to listen to sound files while they're coming through your computer, rather than forcing you to wait until after it has downloaded.

surf: When you simply roam through the Web, following links with no specific destination.

T1: A super-fast, super-expensive connection to the Internet that allows you to download at 1.44MB bps.

TCP/IP: Transfer control protocol/Internet protocol. Another method by which computers communicate on the Internet. If you dial up the Internet you use this method.

text reader: A basic program that allows you to write and read text without any special formatting. In Windows, the text reader is called "Notepad."

thread: In newsgroups and message boards, a series of postings that refer to the same subject heading.

upload: This is the action of transferring files from your computer to another computer.

URL: Uniform resource locator. This is simply the "address" of a Web page, using the "http://" that you type in order to access Web pages.

Usenet: A system that exists on the Internet that contains thousands of newsgroups, on which users post and reply to messages and articles.

viewer: Software that allows you to "view" data on the Internet that contains data that won't appear just as text.

VRML: A programming language that allows you to view virtual reality on the Web.

WAV file: An audio file format that you must download before playing. The file size is relatively small and is used all over the Web.

Web page: A document you can view on the World Wide Web.

Zip file: A file archive that consists of multiple compressed files. Used for faster downloads and storage.